S0-BBH-133

AFFECTIVE
EXPRESSIONS
IN
JAPANESE

A Handbook of Value-Laden Words
in Everyday Japanese

by

RONALD SULESKI

Director,
Asian Regional Program Development
Council on International Educational Exchange, Tokyo Office

and

MASADA HIROKO

Association for Japanese-Language Teaching

THE HOKUSEIDO PRESS

Copyright © 1982 by The Hokuseido Press

Published by The Hokuseido Press
3-32-4, Honkomagome, Bunkyo-ku, Tokyo

INTRODUCTION

Affective expressions are short words or phrases which impart a particular nuance to the sentences in which they are used.

All languages have affective expressions which help to enrich communication by implying subtle differences, such as varying degrees of annoyance or resignation, skepticism or humor. Native speakers of a language use these expressions all the time to flavor their speech. They are usually quick to realize the implication of the affective expression, and they often act on it rather than on the direct meaning of the sentence. A large number of affective expressions are not slang terms, but are standard words used by every native speaker. Native speakers of English use words such as "I *really* can't help you now," or "that was a *stupid* thing to do," as value-laden terms which fall into the category of affective expressions because of the strong nuances they imply.

The Japanese language has a large number of affective expressions which are used in this manner. In most cases non-native speakers of Japanese who are studying the language fail to learn these expressions because they concentrate instead on learning the proper use of grammatical particles and the complex system of conjugating verbs. This is unfortunate since these expressions are in common use and are very important in accurate communication. Once the student of Japanese learns some of these expressions, they will be surprised to discover how often native speakers of Japanese employ affective expressions in both formal and informal communication.

Grammatically these expressions are easy to use. Most act as adverbs and are simply inserted into sentences as independent units which do not take any special grammatical particles. Placing them properly within a sentence is also uncomplicated, because they usually appear just before the word or phrase to which they refer. That is to say, the portion of the sentence following the affective expression contains the idea which is being emphasized.

Thus beginning students of Japanese who have a command of only a few basic sentence patterns can insert affective expressions where appropriate to greatly improve the quality of their speech. More advanced students of Japanese will find that the use of suitable affective expressions in more complex exchanges will give a texture to their speech that will increase their fluency much more effectively than simply expanding their vocabulary of basic terms. The use of these expressions will also allow them to communicate on a level which conveys subtlies and nuances, a level which is extremely important in adult communication.

In spite of the frequency with which affective expressions are used, and their importance to the Japanese language, it is almost impossible to find adequate explanations of their use and the nuances they carry. Most Japanese-English dictionaries give only single word translations of these terms, which rarely convey their full flavor and which usually fail to indicate their proper usage in Japanese social and cultural settings. Word and phrase lists for students of Japanese often omit these expressions to concentrate instead on subject-object-verb combinations which are more directly translatable into English. The problem which such publications are avoiding is the difficulty of giving simple translations for words which carry a range of meanings, and which are dependent upon particular types of social situations for their proper usage.

Therefore this handbook of affective expressions in Japanese has been prepared to help explain the social and cultural situations in which the expressions should be used, and to indicate the full range of English language equivalents for each expression.

This handbook is especially arranged for speakers of English who are students of Japanese, either at the beginning or advanced level, who wish to improve their Japanese language ability. The handbook contains fifty-one expressions arranged in alphabetical order which are commonly used in contemporary written and spoken Japanese. Each expression, given first in romanization and then in its kana version, is followed by a number of English words containing some of the meanings of the expression. An English language explanation of the types of nuances implied by the expression and the categories of situations in which it can be used then appears. This explanation focuses on the cultural, sociological, and sometimes linguistic factors which determine the expression's proper use, although it also contains grammatical explanations when needed and occasionally comments on situations when the expression is best avoided.

Each explanation is followed by a number of example sentences which, if the student desires, can be memorized as a way of increasing both vocabulary and basic patterns, since each example contains a correct usage of the affective expression being explained. The example sentences are given first in kanji / kana, followed by romanization for students whose knowledge of spoken Japanese is stronger than their knowledge of written Japanese.

An English language translation which attempts to capture the nuances of the Japanese expression appears next. The affective expression in the Japanese romaji versions of the sentences as well as its English language equivalents are always indicated in special type. Occasionally the English language word which best conveys the nuance of the affective expression used in a particular sample sentence is not one of the words listed at the beginning of the section as a possible translation. In such cases the student will see how a sometimes wide range of words must be used to indicate to a native speaker of English the correct nuance of the Japanese expression. The English language translations of all sentences represent the conversational, but standard speech which would probably be used by a native speaker of American English. In cases where an expression has several implied meanings, each category of meaning is dealt with in a sub-section under the expression, and each subsection has its own explanation and example sentences.

In preparing the sample sentences, every attempt was made to produce Japanese language sentences which were adult in tone and content. Some of the sentences reflect contemporary concerns while others might naturally appear in almost any Japanese language conversation. All of them could be appropriately used by high school and university students as well as by full adult members of society. Sentences with unusual subject matter or which contained infrequently used grammatical structures were avoided, so the non-native Japanese speaker can be assured that the sample sentences represent standard, conversational, contemporary usage.

The Japanese language sample sentences employ all levels of politeness, from very informal to very polite. At times they are presented in what is known as the written style of contemporary Japanese as well. Teachers can use these various styles of politeness to illustrate to their students how these styles are used in Japan, while students who are unfamiliar with the levels of speech can use the Japanese language sample sentences to improve their ability to comprehend how the several levels of politeness are commonly used.

The English language translation of each sample sentence was of course designed to accurately convey the content of the sentence, but even more so its goal was to capture the nuance contained in the sentence. Because of this, the English language translations do not provide a word-for-word translated version of each sentence, but instead use wording which most accurately conveys the nuance of the sentence in words which a native American English speaker would find most natural. In a number of cases alternate translations of a sample sentence might be possible. Teachers and students using this as a textbook will find it useful to discuss those cases where other translations might be equally accurate.

Although this handbook has been prepared for English language speakers who are studying Japanese, in fact Japanese speakers who are studying English, particularly those from high school to very advanced levels, should also find it useful. Since they will be familiar with the Japanese language expression being described, they will be able to improve their English by studying the explanation provided for each expression and also be reading the explanations given at the beginning of each sub-section. Since the English language equivalents of each term will be in italics, they will be able to understand the implications of the English language affective expression used in the sample sentences. Moreover, they will find a large number of correct English language sentences of native speaker fluency which they can memorize or use to add to their knowledge of English language sentence patterns.

It is the hope of the authors that both Japanese language teachers and English language teachers will find this handbook useful. We hope it will be used for vocabulary and pattern practice, for pronunciation and intonation drills. Further, it can be used in the classroom as the basis for promoting conversation and discussion among students about the use of proper speech in varying social situations. Which leads to our final hope for this handbook, that it will help to encourage empathy and mutual understanding between the Japanese people and their English speaking friends.

Ronald Suleski, Ph. D.
Director
Asian Regional Program Development
Council on International Educational
Exchange Tokyo Office

Masada Hiroko
Association for Japanese-Language
Teaching, Tokyo

は じ め に

　日本人は日常会話の中で，「やっぱり」，「さすが」，「どうせ」などの表現を好んで使います。これらの語句は，短いうちにもそれ自体に，驚嘆，期待，疑い，ためらい，あきらめ，など話者の微妙な感情を含んでいて，表現全体にある意味合いを持たせ，会話を生き生きとしたものにするのに役立っています。日本人なら誰でも聞いた瞬間，その意味するところを了解するこれらの表現も，日本語を学習する外国人にとっては何のことやら分らず，辞書を引いてもただ通りいっぺんの訳語しか見出せません。また，たとい意味が分っても，いかなる状況で，いかに使ったらよいかを完全に会得するのは至難のわざに近いでしょう。このような表現は，もちろん，どの国の言語にもあることと思われますが，とくに日本語には，話者の感情を含む表現や言外に潜む話者の感情を表わす表現が多いようです。そして，これらの表現の使用が，外国人に日本語習得を困難と思わせる原因のひとつともなっていると考えられます。

「日本語は世界で最も難しい言語のひとつだ」とか，「日本語は非論理的だ」とかいう外国人の言葉をよく耳にします。たしかに日本語は，ほとんどの場合，彼等の母国語とは構造的にも音声的にも全く違います。また，外来語は別として，欧米の諸言語のように他の言語から意味を類推することも不可能です。しかし，これは，日本語が他の言語と異なるということであり，日本語が本質的に難しいということを意味するものではありません。日本語には日本語の論理性があり，そこに日本人の思考があります。このことを理解した上で適切な方法で学習すれば，日本語は決して習得困難な言語ではないと考えます。

　例えば，外国人にはいささか唐突に聞える「やっぱり」にしても，短い語の中に凝縮した意味が込められ，聞く人はその場の状況から，それぞれ，「その後も引き続き」とか，「私が予想していた通り」，「常に考えていたように」，或いは，「世間の人々の意見と同じように」とかいう意味合いを直ちに汲みとることができます。そして，外国人学習者に対しても，このような語が発せられるに至る話し手の思考過程，それぞれの持つ意味合い，

発話における状況などの説明があれば，かなり理解可能となり，学習も容易になると思われます。現在に至るまで，この分野の研究・分析は日本語専門家の手によってなされてはいますが，外国人学習者のために，特に書かれた参考書はあまり見当らないようです。

　外国人の日本語学習を容易なものとする仕事の手初めとして，まず，日本人の感情的表現を扱うこととし，今回は，その中から，とりあえず，51の語句を選びました。それぞれの語句には例文を示し，英文による翻訳および解説を付しました。ひとつの語句がふたつ以上の意味を持つ場合には，番号をつけ，各々に意味・例文を示しておきました。なお，例文の日本語には，漢字かな混り，ローマ字の両表記法を用いました。

　この種の語句は，簡単に文中に挿入して使うことができますので，上級の学習者はもとより，基礎の段階を終えた学習者が「日本語らしい日本語」を話す上でも，大いに役立つものと確信いたします。日本語を学習する外国人諸氏が，日本語を通じて日本および日本人を理解するために，この小冊子が何らかの形で，有効な手助けとなるよう願ってやみません。

　ついでながら，この小冊子は，外国人諸氏のための日本語学習の手引きとしてのみでなく，日本人学生諸氏が英語を学習する際の参考としても活用していただければ幸いです。

国際教育交換協議会
アジア地域企画事務所所長
　ロナルド・スレスキー

国際日本語普及協会会員
　政　田　寛　子

TABLE OF CONTENTS

付: ローマ字表記法

1. ローマ字は標準式（修正ヘボン式）を採用する。

2. 長母音は母音文字の上に ‾ を付す【例: dōse, sōtō】。
   ただし，このうち i 音は ii，漢字熟語の e 音は ei と記す【例: ii（好い，良い）; katei, keiei（家庭, 経営）】。

3. 一音節休止のつまる音は後に来る子音を重ねて示す【例: kitto, yappari】。
   ただし，ch, sh, ts 音はそれぞれ，tch, ssh, tts のように記す【例: matchi, zasshi, yattsu】。

4. 鼻音 n は，p, b, m 音の前では m とする【例: sampo, shimbun, hommei】。
   鼻音 n の後に母音または y 音 n 音が来る場合，n 列音との混同を避けるため ′ で節の区切りを示す【例: han′i, ren′ai, hon′yaku; han′nin, don′na】。

Akumade あくまで completely, totally, stubbornly, to the last

EXPLANATION: In its basic meaning, **akumade** means *complete* or filled up. In referring to responsibility, for example, it means to take responsibility *completely*. As an affective expression, it is used to indicate some action that is *complete* or *total*, or tenaciously held, or one that will continue *to the very end*. A sense of being stubborn or *determined* is conveyed by this expression, which is really a logical extension of its basic meaning.

SECTION A   Typical Usages

Illustrated below are examples of the expression **akumade** in which its basic meaning is clearly retained.

EXAMPLES

1. 自分 の 言動 には あくまで 責任 を取らなければ なりません。
   Jibun no gendō ni wa akumade *sekinin o toranakereba narimasen.*

   You must take responsibility *completely* for your own words and actions.

2. 事件 の 容疑者 はあくまで 「自分 は 白 だ」 と 言い張っている。
   Jiken no yōgisha wa akumade *"Jibun wa shiro da" to ii-hatte iru.*

   The suspect in the case *stubbornly* protested saying, "I am totally innocent."

3. 私たち 住民 は高層ビルの 建設 にあくまで 反対 です。
   Watakushitachi jūmin wa kōsō-biru no kensetsu ni akumade *hantai desu.*

   We local residents are *absolutely* opposed to the construction of the high-rise building.

SECTION B   Individual Opinion Expressed

This section illustrates how the expression is used when someone is expressing a personal opinion. Note that in such cases the typical Japanese usage is to end the statement with a *ga*. This indicates some reserve on the part of the speaker and it provides a chance for the listener to respond.

EXAMPLES

4. これ は あくまで　私　の　個人的 な 意見です が。
   Kore wa akumade *watakushi no kojin-teki na iken desu ga.*
   Well, this is *purely* my personal opinion.

5. あくまで仮定 と して 言っている の です が。
   Akumade *katei to shite　itte　iru no desu ga.*
   This is *simply* an assumption on my part.

6. あくまで想像に すぎませんが。
   Akumade *sōzō ni sugimasen ga.*
   This is *nothing more than* a guess.

Dōse　どうせ　　after all,　of course,　anyway,　at any rate,
　　　　　　　　　anyhow

EXPLANATION: **Dōse** is used to signal the conclusion whicn can be
drawn from an informal discussion, or from a long thought process.
It does not mean the conclusion was purposely drawn, but rather
that regardless of how the matter was considered, this seems to be
the conclusion inevitably reached. There is a slight tone of resignation in the expression, and the feeling that the result was ines-
capable (as shown in Section A). In its broadest application (in
Section B), it means "Since you are doing A anyhow, why not also
do B?" In can also be used to imply that the listener agrees with
the logic of the speaker and reaches the same conclusion (as is
illustrated in Section C).

SECTION A　Tone of Resignation
As shown below, the expression **dōse** indicates that a conclusion is
being accepted, although with a sense of resignation on the part
of the speaker.

EXAMPLES

1. どうせ彼 に できる はず は ない,　私　が やってしまおう。
   Dōse *kare ni dekiru hazu wa nai, watakushi ga yatte shimaō.*

At any rate, since he won't possibly be able to do it, I'll do it myself.

2. 私　　　がなにを　主張　して　も，どうせ他人には分ってもらえな
   Watakushi ga nani o shuchō shite mo, dōse *tanin ni wa wakatte moraena-*
   いの だ。
   i no da.

   It doesn't matter what I propose, no one understands it *anyhow.*

SECTION B　Broad Application

This is a conversational application of the expression, which indicates a link between actions. A similar feeling can also be detected in the examples given in Section A above.

EXAMPLES

3. どうせ郵便局へ行くのなら切手を買って来てくださいませんか。
   Dōse *yūbinkyoku e iku no nara kitte o　katte　kite　kudasaimasen ka?*

   Since you're going to the post office *anyway,* won't you please buy me some stamps?

4. どうせ日本語を勉強するのなら，　漢字と仮名も覚えたほうが
   Dōse　*Nihongo o benkyō suru no nara,　kanji to kana mo oboeta hō　ga*
   いいですよ。
   ii　desu yo.

   Since you are going to study Japanese *anyhow,* you might as well learn kanji and kana at the same time.

5. 人間　はどうせ死ぬのだから，好きなことをして暮そう。
   Ningen wa dōse *shinu no da kara, suki na koto o shite kurasō.*

   Since all human beings must die *sooner or later,* we might as well spend our time doing things we like.

SECTION C　Agree with the Speaker

Dōse can also imply that the listener agrees with the logic of the speaker and reaches the same conclusion.

EXAMPLES

6. A: きみ は ほんとう に ばか だ な。
     Kimi wa　hontō　ni baka da na.

A: You're really dumb, aren't you?

B: どうせ, ぼく は ばか な ん だ。
   dōse,   *boku wa baka na n da!*

B: *For sure,* I'm really dumb!

7. どうせ 私　は ばか なん です。
   Dōse *watakushi wa baka na n desu.*

   Of course, (as you imply) I'm a fool!

Futo ふと   suddenly, unexpectedly, involuntarily, casually

EXPLANATION: **Futo** always refers to a situation involving motion
or action, but the actions it refers to are always involuntary rather
than planned. As shown in Section A, it can refer to a mental
action in which some thought or recollection *unexpectedly* occurs.
Sections B and C show how the expression is used to refer to physical actions which took place in the same unplanned or *involuntary*
manner.

SECTION A   A Sudden Thought
Futo can connote some mental action, usually a thought or recollection which occurred *unexpectedly*.

EXAMPLES
1. テレビ を 見ている うちに, ふと　昔　の こと を 思い出した。
   Terebi o mite iru uchi ni, futo *mukashi no koto o omoidashita.*

   While watching television, I *suddenly* remembered something
   from the past.

2. あれ これ　考え 悩んでいたが, ふと いい アイディア が　頭　に
   Are kore kangae nayande ita ga, futo *ii   aidia   ga atama ni*
   浮んだ。
   ukanda.

   My mind was wandering, when *suddenly* I got a good idea.

3. 推理小説　を 夢中 で 読んでいて ふと 気 が つく と, もう 夜中 の
   Suiri-shōsetsu o muchū de yonde ite futo *ki ga tsuku to, mō yonaka no*

三時 を 過ぎて いた。
san-ji o sugite ita.

I was absorbed in the detective novel when I *suddenly* realized that it was past three o'clock in the morning.

SECTION B An Unexpected Action

When used to refer to some physical action which happened *involuntarily* or instinctively, the expression **futo** is used as shown below.

EXAMPLES

4. ふと 耳 を 澄ますと, 草むら で 鳴く 虫 の 声が 聞こえる。
   Futo mimi o sumasu to, kusamura de naku mushi no koe ga kikoeru.

   I *suddenly* pricked up my ears and coming from the bushes could hear the sound of an insect.

5. 本 から 目を 離して ふと 見ると, 外 に は 雪 が 降って いた。
   Hon kara me o hanashite futo miru to, soto ni wa yuki ga futte ita.

   My eyes wandered from the book, when I *happened* to look up and saw that it was snowing outside.

6. 暗やみ の 中 でふと 手を 伸ばすと, 何か 柔か な もの が
   Kurayami no naka de futo te o nobasu to, nanika yawaraka na mono ga
   指先 に 触れた。
   yubisaki ni fureta.

   In the dark I *instinctively* put out my hand, and felt something soft with my fingers.

SECTION C A Trivial Matter

When used in the phrase **futo shita koto**, the expression **futo** indicates something that is of minor importance or trivial, hence its possible translations as *without knowing it* or *casually*.

EXAMPLES

7. 私たち はふとしたことで 友だち になりました。
   Watakushitachi wa futo shita koto de tomodachi ni narimashita.

   Almost *without knowing it* we became friends.

8. 非常 に 仲 が よかった 二人 が ふと した こと で 別れて しまった。
   Hijō ni naka ga   yokatta futari ga futo shita koto *de wakarete shimatta.*

   The two friends who were so close *casually* drifted apart.

9. ふと した こと が きっかけ で この 仕事 を 始めました。
   Futo shita koto *ga kikkake   de kono shigoto o hajimemashita.*

   I began this job *almost accidentally.*

Hatashite はたして   sure enough, just as I thought,
（果して）   as expected, really

EXPLANATION: In its basic meaning, **hatashite** expresses the sense that something turned out just as had been expected. The way it is used can be divided into two categories, although they are rather similar in meaning. The first indicates something that developed as expected (the basic meaning of the expression), while the second indicates the speaker doubts whether something is *truly* so or is *definitely* the case. It can be seen from all the possible translations given above that most of the meanings overlap to some degree.

SECTION A As Expected

When something has developed just as the speaker thought it would, **hatashite** is used as illustrated below.

EXAMPLES

1. 前 から うわさ されて いた 二人 は, はたして この 春 結婚 する
   Mae kara uwasa sarete ita futari wa, hatashite *kono haru kekkon suru*
   こと に なった。
   koto ni natta.

   Sure enough, those two who have been gossipped about for so long will be getting married in the spring.

2. 朝 から 空模様 が あやしい と 思って いたが, はたして 午後 から
   Asa kara sora-moyō ga   ayashii to omotte ita ga, hatashite *gogo kara*
   雨 が 降り出した。
   ame ga furi-dashita.

   I thought the sky looked threatening in the morning, and *just as I expected* it began to rain in the afternoon.

3. 外地 に いる 友人 から 便り が くる 頃 だ と 思って いた が, はた
   Gaichi ni iru yūjin kara tayori ga kuru koro da to omotte ita ga, hata-
   して 長い 手紙 が 届いた。
   shite *nagai tegami ga todoita.*

   I was thinking it was about time for a letter from my friend
   who is abroad, when *just as I expected* a long letter came.

SECTION B   Implies the Speaker's Doubt

To indicate the speaker doubts whether something is actually so,
the expression is used as in the examples below.

EXAMPLES

4. これ が はたして 一番 いい 方法 か どうか, 結果 を みなければ 分
   Kore ga hatashite *ichiban ii hōhō ka dō ka, kekka o minakereba waka-*
   りません。
   rimasen.

   I won't know whether or not this is *really* the best method
   until I can see the results.

5. 彼 は 忙しい 人 だから,   今日 たずねて も はたして 会える か
   Kare wa isogashii hito da kara,   kyō tazunete mo hatashite *aeru ka*
   どう か 分りません。
   dō ka wakarimasen.

   Since he is so busy, I don't know if we'll *really* be able to
   meet today or not.

6. 野党 が 政権 を 握って も, はたして 期待 通り の 政治 が 行なわれる
   Yatō ga seiken o nigitte mo, hatashite *kitai dōri no seiji ga okonawareru*
   か どうか は 疑問 です。
   ka dō ka wa gimon desu.

   Whether or not the opposition party would *really* be able to
   institute the kind of government hoped for once they got pol-
   itical power is a real question.

Ichiō　いちおう　　generally, by and large, for the time being,
　　　　（一応）　　　for the present

EXPLANATION: When used in a sentence, this expression adds the
nuance that the topic of the sentence is general rather than detailed,
fleeting rather than prolonged, or temporary rather than permanent.
Since the fleetingness it stresses refers to an action, it appears most
commonly just before a verb (see examples 1 and 2), though it can
appear just before the subject (examples 3 and 4).

SECTION A　To Mean Generally

This usage often conveys the meaning that the topic of the sentence
has not been finalized, or that it is being discussed as a generality.
It means *by and large* or *to a certain extent*.

EXAMPLES

1. 私　　　は 日本語 はいちおう 話せます が, 上手 ではありませ
   Watakushi wa Nihongo wa　ichiō　*hanasemasu ga,　jōzu de wa arimase-*
   ん。
   n.

   I can express myself in Japanese *to some extent*, but not very
   well.

2. 歌舞伎 について いちおう 知っていますが,　詳しく　はありませ
   Kabuki ni tsuite　ichiō　*shitte　imasu ga,　kuwashiku wa arimase-*
   ん。
   n.

   Generally speaking, I know about kabuki, but not in any detail.

3. これは あしたの 会議の 議題です。いちおう 目を通しておいてく
   Kore wa ashita no kaigi no gidai desu.　Ichiō　*me o tōshite　oite ku-*
   ださい。
   dasai.

   These are the topics for tomorrow's meeting. Please *just* glance
   over them, would you?

SECTION B　To Mean Temporarily

The meaning of this expression given in Section A above shades off easily into that given in this section. **Ichiō** used in this way means *for the time being,* or *provisionally.*

EXAMPLES

4. 代金 はいちおう 半分 だけ 払って ください。
   Daikin wa   ichiō hambun dake haratte kudasai.

   For now would you please pay half of the cost?

5. いちおう ホテル に 部屋 を 取って, ゆっくり アパート を 探す つも
   Ichiō   hoteru ni heya o   totte,   yukkuri   apāto   o sagasu tsumo-
   り です。
   ri desu.

   For the time being I will have a room in a hotel, and intend to take my time looking for an apartment.

Isso いっそ   had better, would rather

EXPLANATION: This expression indicates a decision has been arrived at as the result of a quick attempt to find a solution to a problem. It means that the solution was reached without having carefully thought over the problem.

EXAMPLES

1. こんな に 苦しむ くらい なら, いっそ 死んでしまいたい。
   Kon'na ni kurushimu kurai nara,   isso   shinde shimaitai.

   If I'm ever reduced to such suffering, I *would rather* die.

2. 日本 に いても あまり おもしろい こと はない, いっそ 外国 へ 行っ
   Nihon ni ite mo amari   omoshiroi koto wa nai,   isso gaikoku e   it-
   てしまおうか。
   te shimaō ka.

   There is nothing very interesting to do if I stay in Japan, I should *probably* move to a different country?

3. 夫: この 家 も 大分 古くなって方々 よごれて きたね。
   Otto: "Kono uchi mo daibu furuku natte   hōbō   yogorete   kita ne."
   妻: いっそ 売ってしまいましょう。
   Tsuma: "Isso   utte   shimaimashō."

Husband: "This house is so old that it's dirty everywhere, isn't it?"

Wife: "*That's right.* Let's sell it."

Iyo-iyo   いよいよ   increasingly, more and more, all the more, still more, at last, finally, soon, about to

EXPLANATION: This expression gives a sense of movement or progress to the topic being discussed in the sentence. It indicates a process, one which is increasing, or growing more definite, or which is gradually coming to a conclusion. It often appears after the subject of the sentence and just before the final verb or verb phrase, a placement which adds to the feeling of the verb undergoing a movement through time. Its meaning is rather broad, as can be seen from the many possible translations given above, and it can be used in a large number of situations, as discussed below. In its broadest sense (discussed in Section E), it refers to an eventuality which may occur at some unspecific time in the future.

SECTION A   To Imply Growing Intensity

In this sense the expression is similar to the Japanese word *masumasu*, and it gives the sense of something that is *gradually* growing in intensity.

EXAMPLES

1. 台風 が 近付く につれて，風 はいよいよ 激しく なって きた。
   Taifū ga chikazuku ni tsurete, kaze wa iyo-iyo *hageshiku natte kita.*

   As the typhoon came closer, the winds got *stronger and stronger.*

2. 国際情勢 は 去年 の 秋 頃 からいよいよ 深刻さ を 増してき
   Kokusai-jōsei wa kyonen no aki goro kara iyo-iyo *shinkoku-sa o mashite ki-*
   た。
   ta.

   Since the autumn of last year, the international situation has grown *more and more* serious.

SECTION B To Imply Certainty

Used on this sense, the expression **iyo-iyo** gives a feeling of
something that is coming to be proved true based on a developing
set of circumstances. It refers to a continuing process that is still
taking shape.

EXAMPLES

3. 大会　の　中止　は いよいよ 間違い ない。
   Taikai no chūshi wa iyo-iyo *machigai nai.*

   It now seems quite *certain* the meeting will be called off.

4. 山田氏　　の　　社長　就任 はいよいよ たしか と なった。
   Yamada-shi no shachō shūnin wa iyo-iyo *tashika to natta.*

   As things stand Mr. Yamada's appointment to the company
   presidency is *quite likely* to take place.

SECTION C To Imply a Sense of Process

This expression can be used to imply a strong sense of process,
and refers to a process either in its beginning or ending stages.
It is similar to the Japanese expression *tsui ni* meaning *finally* or
at last, and also similar to the expression *tō-tō* meaning *after all,*
but these expressions are used to refer to the completion of a process, while **iyo-iyo** refers to a process either in its beginning or
ending stages. In other words, it indicates some process that is in
the beginning stages, has just begun, or will soon draw to a close.

EXAMPLES

5. いよいよ　本格的　　な 冬 がやって きた。
   Iyo-iyo *honkaku-teki na fuyu ga yatte kita.*

   Real winter weather has *finally* arrived.

6. 日本 で の　　　留学生活　　も いよいよ 終ろう と している。
   Nihon de no ryūgaku-seikatsu mo iyo-iyo *owarō to shite iru.*

   My student days in Japan are *at last* coming to an end.

SECTION D About to Start

Used in this sense, the expression **iyo-iyo** refers to some process that is about to begin, and it means *about to be* or *imminently*.

EXAMPLES

7. いよいよ 眠り に 入ろうと した 時， 電話 の ベル が 鳴った。
   Iyo-iyo   nemuri ni hairō   to shita toki, denwa no beru ga natta.

   Just as I was *about to* fall asleep, the telephone rang.

8. いよいよ 出発 する 時 に なって， 切符 を 買っていない ことに
   Iyo-iyo shuppatsu suru toki ni natte,   kippu o katte   inai koto ni
   気 が 付いた。
   ki ga tsuita.

   Just as I was *about to* leave, I noticed I had forgotten to buy
   my ticket.

SECTION E   To Refer to a Future Eventuality

This expression can also be used to indicate some eventuality which
might take place in the future.   In such a case it might be translated
into English as *whatever happens*, or *whatever*.

EXAMPLES

9. これ だけ 貯蓄 が あれば，いよいよ の 時 に も 大丈夫 だ。
   Kore dake chochiku ga areba,   iyo-iyo no toki ni mo daijōbu da.

   As long as I have this much money in savings, I'll be okey *in
   any eventuality*.

10. いよいよ と いう 時 の 準備 に， 携帯食糧 を 買っておいた ほうが
    Iyo-iyo   to iu toki no jumbi ni, keitai-shokuryō o katte   oita   hō ga
    いい です よ。
    ii   desu yo.

    It is a good idea to have provisions prepared for *whatever* might
    occur.

Izure いずれ   which, either way, regardless, in any case

EXPLANATION: The expression **izure** means *which*, or which one
of several, as shown in Section A.   The expression can expand
slightly to alter its meaning, but always within the context of

several options or possibilities. For example, when it becomes **izure mo**, as shown in Section B, its meaning becomes *whichever,* or *both.* When it changes to **izure ni shite mo**, shown in Section C, its meaning becomes *regardless of which,* or *in either case.* These are the three most common usages of the expression **izure.** However, when **izure** is used by itself to refer to a time condition, as shown in Section D, it means *soon* or *in the near future.*

SECTION A Which of Several

This usage calls upon the basic meaning of **izure** to ask *which* of several options is preferred.

EXAMPLES

1. A案 と B案, いずれ を 取る か 検討中 です。
   A-an to B-an, izure *o toru ka kentō-chū desu.*

   Which one to adopt, proposal A or proposal B, is now under consideration.

2. 中国料理　　と 西洋料理 の いずれ が おいしい か を 議論する こと
   Chūgoku-ryōri to Seiyō-ryōri no izure *ga   oishii   ka o giron suru koto*

   は ほとんど 無意味 です。
   wa hotondo muimi desu.

   The question of *which* is better, Chinese or Western food, is almost not worth discussing.

3. 家庭 と 仕事 の いずれ を 優先 させる か で, 彼女 は 今　真剣 に
   Katei to shigoto no izure   *o yūsen saseru ka de, kanojo wa ima shinken ni*

   悩んで いる。
   nayande iru.

   She is perplexed about *which* she should give priority to, a home or an outside job.

SECTION B Whichever

The expression **izure mo** is used to mean *whichever* or *either one.* It is similar to the Japanese expressions *dochira mo* and / or *dore mo,* which also mean *whichever* or *either one.* **Izure mo** can also be translated as *both,* since it indicates an acceptance of two things.

EXAMPLES

4. 両力士 いずれ も 十四勝 で 千秋楽 に 出場 した。
Ryōrikishi izure mo *jūyon-shō de senshūraku ni shutsujō shita.*

After two wrestlers got fourteen victories, *both of them* took part in the last day of the sumō matches (Senshūraku).

NOTE: This means that both of the sumō wrestlers were undefeated during the previous fourteen days of the sumō tournament and the two undefeated wrestlers faced each other in the fifteenth, or final day of the tournament.

5. 日本 では 春 と 秋 はいずれ も 気候 が 温和 で 暮し やすい。
Nihon de wa haru to aki wa izure *mo kikō ga onwa de kurashi yasui.*

Living is easy in Japan in *both* the spring and autumn when the temperatures are mild.

SECTION C Regardless of Which

The expression **izure ni shite mo** means *regardless of which one,* or *whatever* the outcome, *or either way.*

EXAMPLES

6. 「イエス」か「ノー」か, いずれ に して も 決定 次第 お知らせしま
"Iesu"   ka "Nō" ka,   izure *ni shite mo kettei shidai oshirase shima*
す。
su.

I will let you know as soon as I decide, *regardless of whether* the answer is yes or no.

7. あした は 仕事 の 都合 でうかがえる か どう か 分りませんがいず
Ashita wa shigoto no tsugō de ukagaeru   ka dō ka wakarimasen ga izu-
れ に して も お電話 します。
re ni shite mo o-denwa shimasu.

Depending on tomorrow's workload, I don't know if I can see you or not, but *in either case* I'll give you a call.

SECTION D Soon or Someday

When referring to time, **izure** indicates either the *near future,* shown in examples 8 and 9 below, or it indicates some point in the future *someday*, as shown in examples 10 and 11. The expression indicates that the exact date cannot be set, but the speaker hopes it will be soon.

EXAMPLES

8. いずれ近いうちにうかがいます。
   Izure *chikai uchi ni ukagaimasu.*

   I'll come to see you *sooner or later.*

9. いずれ お目に かかって 詳しく　　ご説明　いたします。
   Izure *o-me ni kakatte kuwashiku go-setsumei itashimasu.*

   I'll explain in detail when we meet *one of these days.*

10. 犯行 は 隠していても，いずれ 発覚 するに 違いない。
    Hankō wa kakushite ite mo, izure *hakkaku suru ni chigai nai.*

    The crime will be uncovered *someday* regardless of how it's concealed.

11. この　静か な 村 にも，いずれ(は)都市化の 波 が 押し寄せて
    Kono shizuka na mura ni mo, izure *(wa) toshi-ka no nami ga oshiyosete*
    くるの だ。
    kuru no da.

    Even in this quiet village, the wave of urbanization will *someday* sweep in.

Jitsu ni　じつに　　really, very
（実に）

EXPLANATION: The usage and meaning of this expression should be quite clear to speakers of English because its meaning corresponds closely with the English translation given above. It is placed either at the beginning of a sentence or just before the final, or emphasized, portion of a sentence as a way of emphasizing that the information following the expression is true, or accurate, or sincerely given. The expression **jitsu ni** modifies the adverb or adjective which follows it somewhere in the sentence. For example, in sentence No. 1 the **jitsu ni** (*really*) refers to *konde iru* (*heavy* or *crowded*), meaning it is the traffic which is *really* heavy.

EXAMPLES

1. じつに 道 が混んでいますね。
   Jitsu ni *michi ga konde imasu ne.*

   Traffic is *really* heavy, isn't it?

2. 山田さん は 親切 でじつにいい人ですね。
   Yamada-san wa shinsetsu de jitsu ni *ii hito desu ne.*

   Mr. Yamada is kind, and is a *really* fine person, isn't he?

3. じつに面白い 映画でした。最後まで 息もつけない ほど でした。
   Jitsu ni *omoshiroi eiga deshita. Saigo made iki mo tsukenai hodo deshita.*

   That was a *really* interesting movie. I was absorbed in it until it was over.

Jitsu wa   じつは   in fact, really, honestly, truely
              （実は）

EXPLANATION: The expression **jitsu wa** has two broad usages. The first is based on its literal meaning, that of confirming the truth or correctness of some piece of information. When used in this manner, the speaker is confirming or asserting that what follows is *in fact* the actual situation, as shown in Section A. The second usage, as shown in Section B, carries with it a somewhat polite implication. It means the speaker is displaying some reserve (considered a very polite trait among the Japanese) in making the statement which follows the expression in the sentence.

SECTION A To Confirm a Fact
When the correctness, accuracy or truth of something is emphasized, the expression **jitsu wa** can be used. It is often used to indicate that an actual situation might be contrary to the commonly held view, in which case the idea following the expression in the sentence is emphasized as the correct view.

EXAMPLES

1. 彼 はごく 平凡 な 人間 だ と 言われている が, じつは非常に
   Kare wa goku heibon na ningen da to   iwarete   iru   ga, jitsu wa *hijō ni*
   すぐれた才能の　持ち主 だ。
   sugureta sainō no mochinushi da.

   He is said to be a rather ordinary person, but *in fact* he is an especially capable man.

2. 社長 は 仕事 には非常に 厳しくて 冷い よう だが, じつは 大
   Shachō wa shigoto ni wa hijō ni kibishikute tsumetai yō da ga, jitsu wa *tai-*
   へん 心 の 優しい 人 である。
   hen kokoro no yasashii hito de aru.

   The boss is very strict about work and seems to be cold-hearted, but *really* he is a warm-hearted person.

3. 二人 の 関係 は大へん 良い ように 見える が, じつはうちでは
   Futari no kankei wa taihen   yoi   yō ni mieru ga, jitsu wa *uchi de wa*
   夫婦げんか ばかり している そう だ。
   fūfu-genka bakari shite iru   sō da.

   On the surface it seems their relationship is very good, but *in fact* that couple does nothing but fight at home.

4. この 会社 はすべて 順調 にいっている ようだが, じつ は 倒産
   Kono kaisha wa subete junchō ni   itte   iru   yō da ga, jitsu wa *tōsan*
   寸前 だという。
   sunzen da to iu.

   The company seems to be completely sound, but I am told that *in fact* they are about to go into bankruptcy.

SECTION B To Express Reservation

Jitsu wa at the beginning of a sentence or phrase, especially when a slight pause is made after the expression is spoken, indicates some degree of reserve on the part of the speaker. It also can mean that the speaker is about to express something that is sincerely meant.

EXAMPLES

5. じつは, 会社 をやめたい と 思います。
   Jitsu wa, *kaisha o   yametai to omoimasu.*

Frankly, I'd like to quit this job.

6. じつは，大切 な 書類をなくしてしまいました。
   Jitsu wa, *taisetsu na shorui o nakushite shimaimashita.*

   To be honest, I'm afraid I lost some important documents.

7. じつは，ちょっと個人的 な 相談があるのですが。
   Jitsu wa, *chotto kojin-teki na sōdan ga aru no desu ga.*

   There is *actually* a private matter I'd like to talk over.

8. じつは，こんど結婚 することにしました。
   Jitsu wa, *kondo kekkon suru koto ni shimashita.*

   I'd like to inform you that we've decided to get married. (In polite Japanese this is a proper way to inform someone of one's forthcoming marriage. The speaker indicates his reserve, even in making this announcement.)

Kekkyoku けっきょく   in the end, consequently, after all,
（結局）   finally, ultimately

EXPLANATION: This expression originated from the Japanese game of *go* in reference to the final play of the game. It retains that sense of finality and near completion in popular usage and indicates something that is in its *final stage,* or it is used to preface a *conclusion* which is the result of some action, thought or set of factors. These two basically similar usages are illustrated below.

SECTION A In the End

A common usage of **kekkyoku** is to refer to something that is in its *final stage,* or *almost done* or nearing completion.

EXAMPLES

1. 三時間 議論を続けたが，けっきょく 結論 は出なかった。
   San-jikan giron o tsuzuketa ga,   kekkyoku *ketsuron wa denakatta.*

   The discussion went on for three hours and *in the end* no conclusion was reached.

2. 高校を出てから 大学 に行くか 就職 するか迷ったが，   結
   Kōkō o dete kara daigaku ni iku ka shūshoku suru ka mayotta ga,   kek-

局　　　進学 に 決めた。
kyoku *shingaku ni kimeta.*

I was perplexed about whether to go on to university or to get a job after leaving high school, but I *finally* decided to go on to university.

3. マラソン が 始まった 時 には 千人 以上 も いたが, けっきょく 最
   Marason ga hajimatta toki ni wa sen-nin ijō mo ita ga, kekkyoku *sai-*
   後 まで 走った のは 八十人 だけ だった。
   go made hashitta no wa hachijū-nin dake datta.

When the marathon began there were over 1,000 people participating, but *in the end* only 80 runners were left.

SECTION B In Conclusion

Kekkyoku is also used as an expression to indicate a conclusion or final result; in that case it immediately preceeds the stated result. This expression is used the same way as the expression *tsumari,* Section A, which is discussed elsewhere in this book.

EXAMPLES

4. あなた の 言っている ことも, けっきょく　私　の意見と 同じ
   Anata no itte iru koto mo, kekkyoku *watakushi no iken to onaji*
   では ありませんか。
   de wa arimasen ka.

   In sum, isn't what you are saying just the same as my opinion?

5. 彼　は非常に 厳しい こと を 言っている が,　　けっきょく 愛情 の
   Kare wa hijō ni kibishii koto o itte iru ga, kekkyoku *aijō no*
   表現　な の です。
   hyōgen na no desu.

   He is always awfully critical about you, but *in fact* that is his way of expressing affection.

6. 二人 の 論争 は, けっきょく お金 の　問題 なの だ。
   Futari no ronsō wa, kekkyoku *o-kane no mondai na no da.*

   Their quarrels are *ultimately* about money.

Kitto　きっと　　probably, most likely, presumably, certainly, surely, no doubt, always

EXPLANATION:　**Kitto** can be used to express either a mild or a definite probability for a situation which the speaker thinks will occur. Grammatically it can appear almost anywhere in a sentence, but it is usually placed just before the word whose meaning is being emphasized.

SECTION A　Mild Implication

Used in this sense, **kitto** is similar to the Japanese expression *tabun*, which indicates a presumption or a probability.

EXAMPLES

1. 今夜　はひどく冷える，あしたはきっと雪になるだろう。
   Kon'ya wa hidoku hieru,　ashita wa kitto yuki ni naru darō.

   It is so cold tonight, it will *probably* be snowing tomorrow.

2. 吉田さん　はまだ来ません，きっと道が混んでいるんでしょう。
   Yoshida-san wa mada kimasen,　kitto michi ga konde iru n deshō.

   Mr. Yoshida hasn't come yet, *most likely* because of heavy traffic.

SECTION B　Definite Implication

When used to express the feeling that a situation is bound to occur, the expression **kitto** becomes similar to the Japanese word *kanarazu*, which means *no doubt* or *surely*. It implies a certainty or definiteness on the part of the speaker, as illustrated in the examples below.

EXAMPLES

3. お酒を飲むと　翌日　はきっと胃の調子が悪い。
   O-sake o nomu to yokujitsu wa kitto　i no chōshi ga warui.

   When I drink sake I *always* have an upset stomach the following day.

4. 手術　さえ受ければ，あなたの病気はきっと直ります。
   Shujutsu sae　ukereba,　anata no byōki wa kitto naorimasu.

If you'll only have this operation you'll *surely* get better.

5. A: 近い うち, また いらっしゃって ください ね。
      Chikai uchi,   mata   irasshatte   kudasai ne.

A: Please come again soon.

B: はい, きっと うかがい ます。
      Hai,   kitto   ukagai masu.

B: Yes, *I will.* (Yes, *for sure.*)

Masaka   まさか   surely not, impossible, absolutely not

EXPLANATION: This expression is always used to indicate a negative response and it gives the sense that a certain happening will not take place. It is placed in the sentence usually just before the word or phrase being emphasized, and the final verb of the sentence almost always has a negative ending.

SECTION A   Implies an Impossibility

The expression can be used to indicate a situation which the speaker asserts will not occur or could not have occurred. The final verb often ends in *nai darō* or *hazu ga nai*, indicating the speaker's feeling of improbability. It can sometimes be used alone as a reply to a statement, as in a case where one person says, "I saw Nagai-san on the Ginza yesterday," and the listener replies simply, "**Masaka!**" (*Impossible!*)

EXAMPLES

1. まさか あの 人 が そんな ばか な こと を する はず が ない。
   Masaka *ano hito ga sonna baka na koto o suru hazu ga nai.*

   Surely he won't do something that bad.

2. 彼女 は きのう 新婚旅行 に 出かけた の だ から, まさか 東京 に は
   Kanojo wa kinō shinkon-ryokō ni dekaketa no da kara, masaka *Tōkyō ni wa*
   いない でしょう。
   inai deshō.

   Since she left on her honeymoon yesterday, it's *impossible* that she would be in Tokyo.

SECTION B   Against Common Sense

This expression can also imply an assertion that a situation cannot take place because of circumstances, or it cannot take place because it is opposed to common sense, i.e. we cannot afford to let it happen because we fear the consequenses.

EXAMPLES

3. お金 がないからといって，まさか他人 の お金 を 使う わけ に
   O-kane ga nai kara to itte,   masaka tanin no o-kane o tsukau wake ni
   は いかない。
   wa ikanai.

   Even if I have no money of my own, I *cannot* use anyone else's money.

4. 野球 を 見たい が，まさか 会社 を 休んで行く こと は できない。
   Yakyū o   mitai ga,   masaka kaisha o yasunde iku koto wa dekinai.

   I'd like to see a baseball game, but I *cannot* take off from work.

SECTION C   Some Eventuality

This expression is also used to refer to an event that might possibly occur at some unspecific time in the future. Such an event might be a fire, an earthquake, a war or even the collapse of society. All these could occur, though exactly when is unknown. The examples below show how the expression is used in this broad sense.

EXAMPLES

5. 子供 は まさか の 時 に も 困らない ように，強い 人間 に 育
   Kodomo wa masaka no toki ni mo komaranai yō ni, tsuyoi ningen ni soda-
   てたい もの です。
   tetai   mono desu.

   Children should be raised to be strong people who can *overcome* any difficulty.

6. まさか の 時 に 備えて，食料品 は 一週間分 ぐらい 余分 に 買
   Masaka no toki ni sonaete, shokuryōhin wa isshūkan-bun gurai yobun ni ka-
   って おいた ほう が いい です よ。
   tte   oita   hō ga   ii desu yo.

In order to prepare for an *emergency*, it would be a good idea to have an extra week's supply of food.

7. まさか の 時 に は, この 鞄 だけ 持って うち を 出る つもり です。
   Masaka no toki ni wa, kono kaban dake motte uchi o deru tsumori desu.

   When the *emergency* comes, I plan to just grab this bag and run out of the house.

Masa ni まさに　　surely, certainly, really, just, about to,
（正に・将に）　　exactly

EXPLANATION:　The expression **masa ni** can be used in two major ways. It can be used in the assertive sense, as discussed in Section A (正に **masa ni**), to declare that something is *surely* or *certainly* so. Section B (将に **masa ni**) discusses how it is used in a time sense, to refer to something that is on the point of action, and it can be translated as *just as* or *about to*.

SECTION A　（正に **masa ni**)　Assertive Usage
When used in this sense, the expression **masa ni** is similar to the Japanese expression *hontō ni* (really, honestly).

EXAMPLES
1. 私　　が 言いたかった の は, まさに その こと です。
   Watakushi ga iitakatta no wa, masa ni *sono koto desu.*

   What I wanted to say was *exactly* that.

2. 富士山 は まさに 日本一　美しい　山 と 言える でしょう。
   Fujisan wa masa ni *Nippon-ichi utsukushii yama to ieru deshō.*

   Surely we can say that Mt. Fuji is *certainly* Japan's most beautiful mountain.

3. 頂上 から の 眺め は まさに 一幅 の 名画 の よう だ。
   Chōjō kara no nagame wa masa ni *ippuku no meiga no yō da.*

   The view from the summit looks *just* like a beautiful painting.

SECTION B　（将に **masa ni**)　In Reference to Time
When used in reference to time, **masa ni** indicates something that

is at the point of action.

EXAMPLES

4. プラットホームに駆け付けると，電車のドアは まさに締まると
   Purattohōmu   ni kaketsukeru to, densha no doa wa masa ni *shimaru to-*
   ころだった。
   koro datta.

   The train door was *just about to* close as I rushed onto the
   platform.

5. 大統領 は 今 まさに飛行機のタラップを降りるところ です。
   Daitōryō wa ima masa ni *hikōki no tarappu o oriru tokoro desu.*

   The president is *about to* descend from the ramp of the plane.

6. 勇敢 な 消防士は まさに焼け落ちようとしている 家の 中 に
   Yūkan na shōbōshi wa masa ni *yakeochiyō to shite iru ie no naka ni*
   飛び込んで子供を救い出した。
   tobikonde kodomo o sukui-dashita.

   The brave fireman rescued the child by jumping into the house
   just as it was about to be engulfed in flames.

Masashiku まさしく   certainly, surely, no doubt

EXPLANATION: **Masashiku** is used exactly as the Japanese expression *masa ni* (which is also discussed in this book) when it is
used to express something that is true or honestly stated. In those
cases it might be translated as *truly*, *really* or *positively*, in addition
to the possible translations given above. Compare the sentences
below with those given under *masa ni* (1). (Please note that **masashiku** cannot be used to replace *masa ni* as it is illustrated in
Masa ni in Section B. That is to say, **masashiku** cannot be used
to express a time condition.)

EXAMPLES

1. これこそまさしく   私   が長い 間 探していた本です。
   Kore koso masashiku *watakushi ga nagai aida sagashite ita hon desu.*

   That is *exactly* the book I've been searching for for a long time.

2. 彼女 は まさしく 典型的 な 日本人 と 言えます。
Kanojo wa masashiku *tenkei-teki na Nihonjin to   iemasu.*

We could *certainly* call her a typical Japanese.

3. 私   が 言いたかった の は まさしく その こと です。
Watakushi ga   iitakatta   no wa masashiku *sono koto desu.*

What I wanted to speak about was *exactly* that.

4. 富士山 は まさしく   日本一   美しい   山 と 言える でしょう。
Fujisan wa masashiku *Nippon-ichi utsukushii yama to   ieru   deshō.*

We can say that Mt. Fuji is *surely* Japan's most beautiful mountain.

Mashite まして   even more, still more, much more,
definitely less, even fewer, still less

EXPLANATION: **Mashite** is usually used in sentences composed basically of two statements or two parts. It is placed just before the second part of the sentence to indicate that the statement or part which follows it is being emphasized. Most commonly, the speaker will be comparing two conditions and emphasizing the latter one. When used with a negative verb, the *still more* of its basic meaning changes to *still less*.

SECTION A Still More
Mashite can be used to express a condition that is *still more* or *even more* than something else. That is to say, when a generalized statement is made, it can be compared to a more specific statement which follows. By using the expression **mashite**, the second portion of the statement is emphasized. Both the original statement and the emphasized statement, in this usage, express typical or common ideas.

EXAMPLES

1. 私   は まだ 日本語 が 少し しか 話せません，まして   新
Watakushi wa mada Nihongo ga sukoshi shika hanasemasen, mashite *shim-*

聞 や 雑誌 が 読める はず は ありません。
bun ya zasshi ga yomeru hazu wa arimasen.

I can only speak a little Japanese now, so *certainly* I cannot read newspapers or magazines.

2. あの へん は 昼間 も 大へん 静か な 所 です。 まして 夜 は
Ano hen wa hiruma mo taihen shizuka na tokoro desu,   mashite *yoru wa*
寂しい くらい です。
sabishii kurai desu.

This district is always quiet during the daytime. It is *even more* deserted at night. (Literally: It feels quite lonesome at night.)

SECTION B Definitely More, Still Less

This usage of **mashite** is similar to that given above in Section A, except that usually an extreme and a common condition are being compared. When used in this manner, the topic of the first half of the sentence is set off by being followed by the particle *sae* or *demo*. This usage might be expressed by the formula *nani-nani (something) sae* (or *demo*)..., **mashite**...*hazu wa nai*. Sentences following this formula tend to end with negative verbs.

EXAMPLES

3. 我々   は 貧乏 で 食事 さえ 満足 に 取れない の です, まして
Ware-ware wa bimbō de shokuji sae manzoku ni torenai no desu, mashite
自分 の 家 を 持つ など とても 不可能 です。
jibun no ie o motsu nado totemo fukanō desu.

We are so poor we never get enough to eat, so we are *much too* poor to own our own home.

4. 動物   でも 自分 の 子 を かわいがります, まして 人間 の 親 が
Dōbutsu demo jibun no ko o kawaigarimasu,   mashite *ningen no oya ga*
子供   が かわいく ない はず は ありません。
kodomo ga kawaiku nai hazu wa arimasen.

Even some animals love their offspring, so it stands to reason that human parents would love their children *more*.

Masu-masu　ますます　　still more,　more and more,
（増す増す）　increasingly

EXPLANATION: The expression **masu-masu** indicates something that is increasing in intensity or getting progressively stronger. When used with a positive verb, the growing intensity has a positive connotation, and when used with a negative verb, it has a negative connotation. It is similar to the Japanese expression *sara ni* (*more, further*), as it is discussed elsewhere in this book; see *Sara ni*, Section A.

EXAMPLES

1. 夜 に なると 雨 は ますます 激しく なった。
   Yoru ni naru to ame wa masu-masu *hageshiku natta.*

   When it became night the rain got *even* heavier.

2. 日本 と 中国 との 交流 は, 今後 ますます 盛んになること
   Nippon to Chūgoku to no kōryū wa, kongo masu-masu *sakan ni naru koto*
   でしょう。
   deshō.

   Contacts between Japan and China will really *increase* from now on.

3. 今年 初め から 地価 が また 上がり始め, 郊外 に 自分 の 家を 持
   Kotoshi hajime kara chika ga mata agari-hajime, kōgai ni jibun no ie o mo-
   つ という 庶民 の 夢 は ますます 難しく なってきた。
   tsu to iu shomin no yume wa masu-masu *muzukashiku natte kita.*

   Land prices have risen again since the beginning of the year, and the dream of people to have their own home in the suburbs is getting *increasingly* more difficult to realize.

Mazu　まず　　to begin with,　first of all,　in the first place,
now,　well,　probably,　I suppose

EXPLANATION: The ways in which the expression **mazu** is used can be divided into two major categories. Very frequently it is

used to indicate the start or beginning of an explanation or an
action (sentences No. 1 and 2), though it can also mean something
that is the first in a series (sentence No. 3). A second major usage
is to express a possibility, something that is likely to happen, based
on one's first reaction to a situation. For example, to see a cloudy
sky and expect rain (as shown in Section B, sentence No. 4).

SECTION A　To Indicate the Beginning

When used in this sense, **mazu** can be literally translated with such
English language expressions as *to begin with* or *in the first place.*
Quite often, however, it is used by the Japanese as a simple interjection which could be translated as *now* or *well*, though it still
indicates the beginning of an explanation or action.　In both sentences No. 1 and 2 below, either the more specific (*in the beginning*)
or the weaker (*well*) translations would be suitable.

EXAMPLES

1. まず, 自己紹介 をしたい と 思います。
   Mazu, *jiko-shōkai o　shitai　to omoimasu.*
   To begin with, I'd like to introduce myself.

2. まず, 事件 当初 からの 経過報告 をいたします。
   Mazu, *jiken tōshō kara no keika-hōkoku o　itashimasu.*
   First of all, I will give a report on the incident since its very
   beginning.

3. 日本 の 美しい　山 として 挙げられる のは,　まず 富士山 で
   Nihon no utsukushii yama to shite　agerareru　no wa,　mazu Fujisan de-
   しょう。
   shō.

   When considering the most beautiful mountains in Japan, we
   should *begin with* Mt. Fuji.

SECTION B　To Express a Probability

When used to express a possibility, a probability or supposition,
mazu conveys a strong, almost definite, suggestion that something
will probably happen.　It might in such cases be translated as *surely*

or *definitely*, which have a strong meaning.

EXAMPLES

4. 今夜 は 雲 が 多いから，あしたは まず 雨 が 降る でしょう。
   Kon'ya wa kumo ga ōi kara, ashita wa mazu *ame ga furu deshō.*

   Since it's so cloudy tonight, it will *probably* rain tomorrow.

5. 近い うち 東日本 に 大きい 地震 が 起こる ことは まず 間
   Chikai uchi Higashi-Nihon ni ōkii jishin ga okoru koto wa mazu *ma-*
   違い ない だろう。
   chigai nai darō.

   I suppose it's certain that there will be a big earthquake in
   eastern Japan in the near future.

6. 長い 歴史 から 見て，人類の 争い が 全く なくなる ことは
   Nagai rekishi kara mite, jinrui no arasoi ga mattaku nakunaru koto wa
   まず 期待 できない だろう。
   mazu *kitai dekinai darō.*

   Considering what we know of human history, *I guess* there is
   no hope that human beings will ever stop fighting.

Mushiro　むしろ　　　rather, would sooner

EXPLANATION: **Mushiro** is an expression which implies that a
comparison has been made between two conditions, objects or options, and that one of them, the latter, has been selected. In the
Japanese sentence it is placed just before the condition or option
which has been selected.

EXAMPLES

1. 今日 は 涼しい という より むしろ 寒い くらい ですね。
   Kyō wa suzushii to iu yori mushiro *samui kurai desu ne.*

   It's not cool, it's cold!　(It's cold *rather* than cool.)

2. こういう 仕事 は 人 に 頼む より むしろ 自分でやってしまう
   Kō iu shigoto wa hito ni tanomu yori mushiro *jibun de yatte shimau*
   ほう が 楽 です。
   hō ga raku desu.

Rather than ask someone to do this kind of job, it will be easier to do it myself.

3. そんな こと を する くらい なら，むしろ死んだほう が いい。
   Son'na koto o suru kurai nara, mushiro *shinda hō ga ii.*

   I *would sooner* die than do that.

Namaji　なまじ　　not fully, not thoroughly, thoughtlessly, incompletely

EXPLANATION: The basic meaning of this expression indicates something that is raw, not fully prepared or not matured. Often placed at the beginning of a sentence or long phrase, this expression implies a negative condition or state. When used in the sense of something that ought to be done, the speaker seems to be giving a warning that a negative result can occur if the required action is *not fully* performed. It also conveys the impression of something done *carelessly* or *not thoroughly*, possibly therefore resulting in a negative condition (as in sentence no. 2). Actually the expression often seems to imply a little bit of both types of meanings when used in conversation.

EXAMPLES

1. なまじ 外国語 を 知っている と かえって 困る こと が ある。
   Namaji *gaikokugo o shitte iru to kaette komaru koto ga aru.*

   Even if you know only *a little bit* of a foreign language, sometimes you're bound to have trouble. (This sentence implies that it might be dangerous to know only a little bit of a foreign language.)

2. なまじ言い訳をすると かえって 誤解 を 招く　恐れ が ある。
   Namaji *iiwake o suru to kaette gokai o maneku osore ga aru.*

   You had better not make an *incomplete* explanation because it could result in a misunderstanding. (The implication of the expression as it is used here is stronger than that in the sentence above.)

3. 病人 が なまじ 医学 の 本 など 読む と かえって 心理的 に 悪い
   Byōnin ga namaji *igaku no hon nado yomu to kaette shinri-teki ni warui*
   影響 が ある。
   eikyō ga aru.

   A sick person *should be careful* about reading medical books,
   because the books are bound to have a bad psychological effect
   on him. (This sentence implies it might be better for sick
   persons to refrain from reading medical books.)

Omowazu 思わず   instinctively, involuntarily, unintentionally

EXPLANATION: The basic meaning of this expression means something that was not thought about. It is composed of the word
omou (to think) and the negative ending *zu*, which means it was
not thought. As indicated by the possible translations given above,
therefore, it means something that was done without thought or
without being planned; hence it refers to something that happened
instinctively or *involuntarily*. The expression carries no value judge-
ments as to whether the unintentional action was good or bad, but
merely reports its unplanned occurance. Note that the expression
is simply inserted into the sentence as it stands. It is not used as
an adjective and does not take any particles such as *na* or *ni*.

EXAMPLES

1. 大学入試 　合格 の 通知 が 来た 時，　嬉しかったので 思わず
   Daigaku-nyūshi gōkaku no tsūchi ga kita toki,　ureshikatta node omowazu
   「万歳」 と 叫んでしまった。
   "Banzai!" to sakende shimatta.

   When the notice came informing me I had passed the university
   entrance exam, I was so happy I *instinctively* shouted, "Banzai!".
   (As this sentence indicates, the use of the word *banzai* is here
   the equivalent of a cheer such as "hooray".)

2. 重要 な 会議 だった が，彼女 の 　発言 が あまりにも 突飛 だった
   Jūyō na kaigi datta ga, kanojo no hatsugen ga amari ni mo toppi datta

ので 思わず大きな 声で笑ってしまった。
node omowazu *ōki na koe de waratte shimatta.*

It was an important meeting, but what she said was so far off
the topic that I laughed out loud *in spite of myself.*

3. ニュースで知人 の 死 が 報道 された。　予期 しない こと だったの
   Nyūsu   de chijin no shi ga hōdō sareta.   Yoki shinai koto datta no-
   で，思わず持っていた コップを 落して しまった。
   de, omowazu *motte ita koppu o otoshite shimatta.*

The death of my acquaintance was reported on the news, and
since his death was so unexpected, (when I heard the report)
I *involuntarily* dropped the cup I was holding.

Roku ni . . . nai　ろくに . . . ない	almost nothing,
Roku na . . . nai ろくな . . . ない	almost none,
Roku de mo nai ろくでもない	nothing worthwhile,
	nothing satisfactory,
	worthless

EXPLANATION: The expression **roku** means something that is
complete, proper, correct or *satisfactory.* When it is combined with
other particles and a negative verb to become **roku ni . . . nai,**
roku na . . . nai, or **roku de mo nai**, it indicates something that is
insufficient, not worthwhile or *valueless.* This expression unlike the
majority of expressions discussed in this book, is commonly used
with these various particles which are illustrated below.

SECTION A Almost None, Almost Nothing
The expression **roku ni . . . nai** is used to modify a verb, in which
case it carries the idea of *almost none.*

EXAMPLES
1. 最近 は 忙しくて，家 に 帰っても 疲れているので 家内 とろ
   Saikin wa isogashikute, uchi ni kaette mo tsukarete iru node kanai to ro-
   くに 話 も できません。
   ku ni *hanashi mo* dekimasen.

Recently I've been so busy that when I return home I *hardly* speak with my wife because I'm so tired.

2. 世 の 中 に は ろくに 食事 も できない 貧しい 人 が たくさん い
   Yo no naka ni wa roku ni *shokuji mo* dekinai *mazushii hito ga takusan i-*
   る の を 忘れて は なりません。
   ru no o wasurete wa narimasen.

   We must bear in mind that there are many poor people in this world with *almost* nothing to eat.

3. ろく に 教育 も 受けて いない 彼 が 成功した 理由 は どこ に ある
   Roku ni *kyōiku mo* ukete inai *kare ga seikō shita riyū wa doko ni aru*
   の だろう。
   no darō?

   What is the reason that he who has *almost no* education has accomplished so much?

SECTION B   Nothing Worthwhile

The expression **roku na . . . nai** is used to modify a noun. It means that the noun (thing or matter) to which it refers has no value, or that its value is very low. Possible translations are shown below.

EXAMPLES

4. 焼きもの の バーゲン・セールに 行って みましたが， ろくなもの
   Yaki-mono no   bāgen-sēru   ni itte   mimashita ga,   roku na *mono*
   は ありませんでした。
   wa arimasen*deshita.*

   I went to the pottery sale, but there was *nothing worthwhile* for sale.

5. 勉強 も しないで 漫画 ばかり 読んで いる と， ろくな 人間 には
   Benkyō mo shinaide manga bakari yonde iru to,   roku na *ningen ni wa*
   なりません よ。
   narimasen *yo.*

   If you don't study but only read comic books, you *won't turn into* a decent person.

6. ろく な 仕事 も しないで， 給料 を 上げて くれ という のは 間
   Roku na *shigoto mo* shinaide, *kyūryō o agete kure to iu no wa ma-*

違っている でしょう。
chigatte iru　deshō.

If you *don't do any worthwhile* work, you're mistaken to think your pay will be raised.

SECTION C　Worthless

Roku de mo nai is also a version of the basic expression which is used to convey the idea that something has little or no value.

EXAMPLES

7. この 子は ろく でも ない 本 ばかり 読んでいて 困ります。
   Kono ko wa roku de mo nai hon bakari yonde ite komarimasu.
   I'm afraid this child only reads *bad* books.

8. 彼　はろくでもないこと ばかり 言って 人を 笑わせようとする。
   Kare wa roku de mo nai koto bakari itte hito o warawaseyō to suru.
   He always says *something silly* to make people laugh.

9. 主人　はろくでもない 骨董品を 買って きては, ひとりで 喜んで
   Shujin wa roku de mo nai kottōhin o katte kite wa, hitori de yorokonde
   います。
   imasu.

   My husband always buys a *worthless* antique which only he is happy about.

Sara ni　さらに　　　anew, again, further, more, still,
　　　　　（更に）　　（not) at all

EXPLANATION: The expression **sara ni** gives a basic feeling of a situation that is progressing, or a condition that is becoming progressively stronger.　Section A and B illustrate its usage in situations that are progressing, while Sections C and D show how it is used to refer to conditions that are becoming progressively stronger. When used in a sentence, a sense of something continuing and / or intensifying is always conveyed.

SECTION A　Recurring Condition

The expression **sara ni** can be used to refer to a condition that has existed, but is likely to change or continue.

EXAMPLES

1. この 研究 はさらに 続けていくつもり です。
   Kono kenkyū wa sara ni *tsuzukete iku tsumori desu.*

   I intend to continue this research *further.*

2. 豪雨 に よる 被害 は 以上 です。さらに 情報 が 入り 次第 お知らせし
   Gōu ni yoru higai wa ijō desu. Sara ni *jōhō ga hairi shidai o-shirase shi-*
   ます。
   masu.

   The damage caused by the heavy rain is as just reported. You will be informed immediately of any *further* change in the situation.

SECTION B Increasing in Intensity

Sara ni can also be used to indicate a condition that is increasing in intensity, something that began and is getting progressively stronger. The growing intensity can have a positive or a negative connotation.

EXAMPLES

3. 国鉄   は 今年 も 運賃 の 値上げ を しなければ,   赤字 は さら
   Kokutetsu wa kotoshi mo unchin no neage o shinakereba,   aka-ji wa sara
   に 増える と 言っている。
   ni *fueru to itte iru.*

   The Japanese National Railways Corporation said that if they do not raise their passenger and freight charges again this year, they will go *further* in the red.

4. 国際間   の 緊張 は この ままにしておけば, さらに   深刻 に
   Kokusai-kan no kinchō wa kono mama ni shite okeba, sara ni *shinkoku ni*
   なる ばかり だ。
   naru bakari da.

   If international tensions continue as they are, the international situation will only *get worse.*

SECTION C Still More

Besides referring to a continuing process, as illustrated in Sections

A and B above, **sara ni** can also refer to a state of being or a condition, indicating that a particular state or condition is comparatively stronger or more intense than another condition with which it is being compared.

EXAMPLES

5. 日本人 の　　　大学進学率　　も 高い が，　アメリカ人 の それ は
   Nihonjin no daigaku-shingaku-ritsu mo takai ga,　　Amerikajin no sore wa
   さらに 高い。
   sara ni takai.

   The percentage of Japanese who enter university is high, but it is *even higher* for Americans.

6. 彼女　　も 美人 ですが，彼女 の お姉さん は さらに きれい です よ。
   Kanojo mo bijin desu ga, kanojo no o-neesan wa sara ni kirei desu yo.

   She is pretty, but her sister is *even prettier.*

SECTION D   Complete Negative

When used with a negative verb, **sara ni** expresses a strong denial or a complete negation. This is a logical continuation of its uses as illustrated above, except that when used with a negative verb it gives a final, and not a continuing, denial.

EXAMPLES

7. あなた が 正しい の だから，あやまる 必要 は さらに ありません。
   Anata ga tadashii no da kara, ayamaru hitsuyō wa sara ni arimasen.

   Since you are correct, your apology is *totally* unnecessary.

8. あんな こと を した のに，反省 する 気 は さらにない の だから
   An'na koto o shita noni, hansei suru ki wa sara ni nai no da kara
   全く あきれる。
   mattaku akireru.

   I am astounded that although he did that, he has no intention *at all* of reflecting on it.

Sasuga (ni) さすが (に)   naturally, really, indeed,
as expected, truly, even

EXPLANATION: The expression **sasuga ni** is used to underscore or
to emphasize the truth of a particular situation or thought. Most
native American speakers would probably use the word *really* to
add the emphasis, while British speakers or Americans being slightly
more formal, would say *indeed*. This expression is used both in
cases where there is general agreement about the truth of the
statement (see Sections A and B), as well as to accentuate the special
quality of a situation (see Section C). Its use as a noun modifier
is shown in Section D.

SECTION A   To Emphasize a Logical Statement
When a particular situation is explained in the first part of a
sentence and the effect of that situation, as expressed in the second
part of the sentence, is emphasized, the expression **sasuga ni** is
used as illustrated below. The emphasized portion often expresses
an *expected* result.

EXAMPLES

1. 十年 も 勉強 しているというが，さすが に 彼 の 日本語 は 正
   Jū-nen mo benkyō shite iru to iu ga, sasuga ni *kare no Nihongo wa sei-*
   確 だ。
   kaku da.

   Having studied for ten years, *naturally* his Japanese is good.

2. 家庭教育 が 厳しいので，山田さん の 子供たち は さすがに
   Katei-kyōiku ga kibishii node, Yamada-san no kodomo-tachi wa sasuga ni
   礼儀正しい。
   reigi tadashii.

   Because of strict training at home, Mr. Yamada's children have
   really good manners.

3. 専門家 なので，彼 はさすがに現在 の 経済情勢について 深い
   Semmonka na node, kare wa sasuga ni *genzai no keizai-jōsei ni tsuite fukai*

見方 をしている。
mikata o shite iru.

Being a specialist, he *truly* has an extremely knowledgable way
of looking at the current economic situation.

SECTION B   To Emphasize a General Consensus

Sasuga ni can be used to emphasize the truth about a statement
or situation about which everyone generally agrees. Since there is
little disagreement about the truth of the statement, the expression
can also be used by itself to constitute a reply acknowledging
agreement. For example, if A says, "That person's pronunciation
is very accurate and clear," and B answers by saying, "He's an
announcer on NHK, you know," A person can respond by simply
saying, "**sasuga!**" (*Indeed!*) Native American speakers might translate the reply as "*Is that so!*", but in either case the reply indicates
an agreement which emphasizes the truth of A's original statement.

EXAMPLES

4. さすが に 日本 の 富士山 は 美しい。
   Sasuga ni Nihon no Fujisan wa utsukushii.

   Japan's Mt. Fuji is *really* beautiful. (This sentence implies that
   the truth of the statement is generally accepted.)

5. さすが に あの レストラン の ビフテキ は おいしい。
   Sasuga ni ano   resutoran no bifuteki wa   oishii.

   That restaurant's beefsteak is *really* good. (This statement
   implies that the restaurant's beefsteak is famous; it is known
   to be good.)

6. さすが に NHK の アナウンサー は   発音 が いい。
   Sasuga ni NHK no   anaunsā   wa hatsuon ga   ii.

   The announcers at NHK have *really* good pronunciation.

SECTION C   To Give Special Emphasis

As illustrated above, **sasuga ni** is often used in situations where
the emphasized condition represents an expected outcome (Section
A) or where there is general agreement about its truth (Section B).

It can also be used, however, to underline the uniqueness or special quality of a situation. Although used and translated in a similar manner, its meaning becomes slightly stronger in this usage.

EXAMPLES

7. いつも元気な彼も，さすがに今度の病気には参ったらしい。
   Itsumo genki na kare mo, sasuga ni *kondo no byōki ni wa maitta rashii.*

   He is usually so healthy, but because this time his sickness is so bad, he *really* can't overcome it.

8. いつもはっきり物を言う医者だが，さすがにその患者に　直
   Itsumo hakkiri mono o iu isha da ga, sasuga ni *sono kanja ni choku-*
   接　「癌です」とは言えなかった。
   setsu "Gan desu" to wa ienakatta.

   The doctor usually speaks his mind freely, but *indeed*, this time he couldn't tell the patient, "It's cancer." (Note that it is the practice in Japan to not directly tell a cancer victim that he has cancer.)

9. いつもよくできる彼も，さすがにこの　試験問題　だけは解けな
   Itsumo yoku dekiru kare mo, sasuga ni *kono shiken-mondai dake wa tokena-*
   かった。
   katta.

   He can usually do well on tests, but because this time it is a *really* tough problem, he hasn't been able to solve it.

SECTION D Used to Modify a Noun

When **sasuga** is used as a modifier of a noun, a situation which would normally be explicitly expressed, as in Section C above, is instead only implied. A comparison of the example sentences in Section C and Section D will illustrate how this occurs. Used as a noun modifier, the formula is: **sasuga**+*no*+noun.

EXAMPLES

10. さすがの彼も，今度の病気には参ったらしい。
    Sasuga no kare mo, kondo no byōki ni wa maitta rashii.

    Even he can't overcome nis sickness this time.

11. さすが の 医者 も，その 患者 に　　直接　「癌 です」 と は 言えなか

Sasuga no *isha mo, sono kanja ni chokusetsu "Gan desu" to wa   ienaka-*

った。

tta.

Even the doctor couldn't frankly say to the patient, " It's cancer."

12. さすが の 彼 も，この 問題 だけ は 解けなかった。

Sasuga no *kare mo, kono mondai dake wa tokenakatta.*

Even he hasn't been able to solve this problem.

Sei-zei　せいぜい　　　no more than,　at most,　at best,
nothing more,　as far as possible,
as much as

EXPLANATION: The expression **sei-zei** always refers to some volume or amount. Within that limitation it has two negative and one positive usage. In regard to numbers or time or action, it indicates the definite limit which exists in each case; i.e. few numbers, little time or limited action. (Sections A and B illustrate these usages.) However, in its polite usage (see Section C) it refers to reaching the greatest limit possible, or striving to reach the limit. Thus the expression approaches the idea of a limit from two opposite psychological perspectives. On the one hand it stresses the limiting aspect of the set amount, and on the other hand it emphasizes trying to expand to reach the limit.

SECTION A No More Than (Numbers or Time)

In referring to numbers or time, **sei-zei** indicates that the amount of the numbers or time did not exceed the number which follows the expression in the sentence. It means the actual number or time was probably less than the stated figure.

EXAMPLES

1. この 会合 に 集まった のは せいぜい 二十人 だった。

Kono kaigō ni atsumatta no wa　sei-zei　*nijū-nin datta.*

There were *no more* than twenty people at the meeting.

2. 忙しい　ので 本 が 読める のは せいぜい 一日 に 一時間 ぐらい で
   Isogashii node hon ga yomeru no wa sei-zei *ichinichi ni ichi-jikan gurai de-*
   す。
   su.

   Since I've been so busy I've been able to read the book *at most* one hour a day.

3. 日本人　は　夏　の　休暇でも せいぜい 一週間 という のが 普通 で
   Nihonjin wa natsu no kyūka demo sei-zei *isshūkan to iu no ga futsū de*
   ある。
   aru.

   For the Japanese it is usual for summer vacation to be *not more than* one week long.

SECTION B   At Best (Action)

When used to refer to an action, **sei-zei** indicates that the action is not significant, or that the action is *about all* that is performed, with little else performed beyond it.   Thus it points out what is the most prominent point of a basically insignificant action.

EXAMPLES

4. 彼　の日本語 はせいぜい 日常会話 に 困らない だけ です。
   Kare no Nihongo wa sei-zei *nichijō-kaiwa ni komaranai dake desu.*
   His Japanese is *at best* adequate for basic communication.

5. スポーツはせいぜい息子 と キャッチ・ボールをする くらい です。
   Supōtsu wa sei-zei *musuko to kyatchi-bōru o suru kurai desu.*
   As for sports, *about all* I do is play catch with my son.

6. 会社 での　　私　の 仕事 はせいぜい 書類 の 整理をする 程度
   Kaisha de no watakushi no shigoto wa sei-zei *shorui no seiri o suru teido*
   です。
   desu.

   At the office my work consists of *nothing more* than filing papers.

SECTION C   As Far As Possible

Unlike the other two usages of **sei-zei** shown above, in this section the expression is very positive in tone. It means to do something *to the best of* one's ability, or *as far as possible*. In this usage it often appears in conversation and letters.

EXAMPLES

7. 毎日　お忙しい と 思います が, せいぜい 健康 に 気 を 付けて くだ
   Mainichi o-isogashii to omoimasu ga, sei-zei *kenkō ni ki o tsukete kuda-*
   さい。
   sai.

   I know you are busy everyday, but please take *as good care of* your health *as possible*.

8. お国　へ 帰られて も, せいぜい 日本語 を 使って ください。
   O-kuni e   kaerarete mo,   sei-zei *Nihongo o tsukatte kudasai.*

   Even after you return home (to your country), please use Japanese *as much as you can*.

9. また いつ お会い できる か 分りません が, せいぜい 手紙 を 書く つ
   Mata itsu   o-ai   dekiru ka wakarimasen ga,   sei-zei *tegami o kaku tsu-*
   もり です。
   mori desu.

   I don't know when we will meet again, but I intend to write *as much as* I can.

10. 連休　に は どこ へ も 行かないで, せいぜい 休養 する つもり です。
    Renkyū ni wa doko e mo ikanaide,   sei-zei *kyūyō suru tsumori desu.*

    I won't go anywhere during the holidays, but I plan to rest *as much as* I can.

Sekkaku　せっかく   especially, purposely, kindly, ought to,
　　　　　　（折角）   should properly do

EXPLANATION: The basic meaning of **sekkaku** is to convey the idea of some act being *especially* or *purposely* done. It is often used in the sense that although a special effort was made, the desired result was not achieved. In such circumstances it expresses the speaker's disappointment. When used in this manner the formula is **sekkaku**...*no ni* (although)...bad or negative result. Finally, the expression is also used to mean something that *ought to be* done if a desired goal is to be achieved.

SECTION A To Express Regret

This usage refers to a goal which was not realized in spite of special efforts taken or in spite of the wishes of the speaker. The grammatical particle *no ni*, translated as although, often appears in this usage and the expression **sekkaku** can be placed at the beginning of the entire sentence.

EXAMPLES

1. せっかく 手紙 を 書いた のに, 出す の を 忘れて しまった。
   Sekkaku *tegami o   kaita   noni,   dasu no o wasurete shimatta.*

   Although I *especially* wrote the letter for a specific purpose, I forgot to mail it.

2. せっかく いい 職場 を 探して あげた のに, 彼 は 断って しまった。
   Sekkaku *ii shokuba o sagashite ageta   noni, kare wa kotowatte shimatta.*

   I *went to the trouble of* finding him a good job, but he refused to take it.

SECTION B To Be Purposely Done

Sekkaku is sometimes used to mean something that should be *especially* or *purposely* done, otherwise a chance to achieve a desired goal will be lost.

EXAMPLES

3. せっかく ここ まで 来た の だ から, 友人 に 会って 行こう。
   Sekkaku *koko made kita no da kara, yūjin ni atte   ikō.*

   Since I've *especially* come this far, I'm going to meet my friend.

4. せっかく つかんだ 好機 を 逃さない よう に, 大いに がんばろう。
   Sekkaku *tsukanda kōki o nogasanai yō ni,   ōi ni gambarō.*

   In order not to lose this *long-awaited* opportunity, I *must* start trying harder.

SECTION C   To Express Gratitude

Used in this manner, the expression refers to an opportunity that should be taken in order to achieve a desired goal. Grammatically it often takes the form of **sekkaku no**+noun. Using it as a noun modifier tends to simplify the sentence, as can be seen if this section is compared with the examples in Section B above, where the content of the sentences is spelled out in more detail.

EXAMPLES

5. せっかく の ご好意 ですから, いただきます。
   Sekkaku no *go-kōi desu kara,   itadakimasu.*

   This is *especially* kind of you. I gladly accept.

6. せっかく の 休み だから, 家族そろって ピクニックに 出かけま
   Sekkaku no *yasumi da kara,   kazoku sorotte   pikunikku ni dekakema-*
   しょう。
   shō.

   Since we're on vacation, we *ought to* go on a picnic. (This sentence implies that we ought to take the opportunity provided by being on vacation to have a picnic.)

Semete   せめて   at least, at best, at most

EXPLANATION: Basically this expression means that although the ideal result cannot be achieved, *at least* some attempt to realize it is possible. It indicates that the actor's ultimate hope or desire must be limited. Sentences using this expression often contain two basic clauses, the first setting forth the somewhat negative or limiting condition, and the second, often beginning with **semete,** which states the degree of positive action possible. This basic construction is illustrated in the examples below.

EXAMPLES

1. 定年 になる まえ に, せめて自分の家を持ちたい。
   Teinen ni naru mae ni,   semete *jibun no ie o   mochitai.*

Before it becomes time to retire, I want to *at least* own my own home.

2. 毎日　忙しい　日 が　続く　が，せめて　お正月　だけ でも のんびり
   Mainichi isogashii hi ga tsuzuku ga, semete *o-shōgatsu dake demo   nombiri*
   過ごしたい。
   sugoshitai.

   I am busy everyday, but *at least* I want to relax on New Year's Day.

3. 外国語　は 何 も できないが，せめて 英語 だけ でも 習得したい。
   Gaikokugo wa nani mo dekinai   ga, semete *Eigo dake demo shūtoku shitai.*

   I can't speak any foreign language, but I want to learn English *at least*.

Shimi-jimi (to)　しみじみ（と）　　dearly,　sincerely,　fondly, deeply,　yearn for

EXPLANATION: The basic meaning of this expression comes from the verb *shimiru*, which means to *soak* or *penetrate*. Thus **shimi-jimi** is an expression which indicates some emotion or some action that comes from deep within the heart. It conveys a positive heart-felt feeling such as *deep* gratitude. It also expresses a feeling akin to sentimentalism similar in meaning to the Japanese word *natsukashii* (to *long for*, to *yearn for*, to *miss very much*).

EXAMPLES

1. 静か　な 夜 はふるさとのことがしみじみ 思い出される。
   Shizuka na yoru wa furusato no koto ga shimi-jimi *omoi-dasareru.*

   On a quiet night I *fondly* recall my old hometown.

2. 逆境　に いる 時 は，人 の　親切　がとくにしみじみと 感じら
   Gyakkyō ni iru toki wa, hito no shinsetsu ga toku ni shimi-jimi *to kanjira-*
   れる。
   reru.

   In times of adversity one especially feels *deep* gratitude for the kindness of others.

3. 彼　はグラスを片手に，若い日の思い出をしみじみと語った。
Kare wa gurasu o katate ni, wakai hi no omoide　o shimi-jimi to katatta.

He held the glass and *longingly* recalled his youth.

Shimmiri (to)　しんみり（と）　　sentimentally,　quietly,
　　　　　　　　　　　　　　　　　　　intimately,　touchingly

EXPLANATION: **Shimmiri** is used to express deep and profound human emotions. The emotions to which it refers are *longing, yearning for*, being *sad* or *sentimental*. When this word is spoken in a sentence, some of the emotions it conveys can be seen from the tone of voices of the speaker; it is often spoken quietly. It carries with it a feeling of *regret* or *sympathy*, emotions which tend to be passive, quiet and restrained. It is a difficult expression to translate because of the wide range of emotions it refers to and because of the subtly of those emotions.

SECTION A To be Sentimental

As illustrated below, **shimmiri** expresses a feeling of *sympathy, sentimentality*, or of simply being quiet and thoughtful. Note that in the sentences below, when the expression **shimmiri** is written as **shimmiri** (**to**) **shita** or **shimmiri shita**, it acts as a noun modifier. This is how the expression often appears in normal speech.

EXAMPLES

1. あの頃を思い出し，しんみり（と）した　気持　で　この　手紙を書
Ano koro o omoidashi,　shimmiri (to) shita *kimochi de　kono tegami o ka-*
いています。
ite　imasu.

I remember those days and with a *sentimental* feeling am writing this letter.

2. 父親　は　娘　の　　花嫁姿　　をしんみり（と）した　顔つき
Chichioya wa musume no hanayome-sugata o　shimmiri (to) shita *kaotsuki*
で眺めていた。
de nagamete ita.

With a *thoughtful* face the father was staring at his daughter in her bridal gown.

3. 「いよいよ お別れ です ね」 と 彼女 は しんみり (と) した 口調 で 言
   "Iyo-iyo   o-wakare desu ne"   to kanojo wa shimmiri *(to) shita kuchō de i-*
   った。
   tta.

   "Well, it's time to part," she *sadly* said.

SECTION B   To Yearn For

When used in this sense, **shimmiri** is similar in meaning to the Japanese expression *shimi-jimi* (longingly, fondly) which is discussed elsewhere in this book. Note also that the word *to* can be used before the verb or it can be omitted.

EXAMPLES

4. 彼 はなき 母親 の 思い出 をしんみり (と) 話した。
   Kare wa naki hahaoya no omoide o shimmiri *(to) hanashita.*

   He spoke *sadly* when recalling his deceased mother.

5. 彼女 は 寒い 北国 の 宿 で, 恋人 への 慕情 をしんみり (と)
   Kanojo wa samui kitaguni no yado de,   koibito e no bojō o shimmiri *(to)*
   歌っていた。
   utatte   ita.

   In a small inn in the cold north country, she *longingly* sang a song about her devotion to her lover.

Sōtō そうとう   pretty, fairly, tolerably, considerably,
　　（相当）   equivalent, appropriate, proper

EXPLANATION: In its most literal meaning, the expression **sōtō** could be translated to mean that something is equivalent to or corresponds to something else. Thus one can derive the various possible translations given above from its basic meaning. When used as an adverb, as in sentence No. 1 below, the expression is simply inserted as it stands into a sentence at an appropriate point, and sometimes it becomes **sōtō ni,** as in sentences No. 2 and 3.

When used as an adjective, as in sentence No. 4, it becomes **sōtō no** or **sōtō na** and takes the common adjectival ending. It can become a verb also by using it as **sōtō suru**, as in sentence No. 5.

SECTION A   Most Common Usage

The expression is most commonly used as it stands, without taking any particle, and it is used to mean *considerably* or *pretty* (referring to intensity).

EXAMPLES

1. さっき の 地震 は そうとう ひどかった です ね。
   Sakki   no jishin wa   sōtō   *hidokatta   desu ne.*

   That earthquake was *pretty* strong, wasn't it?

2. 敬語 は 母 から そうとう 厳しく 教えられました。
   Keigo wa haha kara   sōtō   *kibishiku oshieraremashita.*

   Mother *very strictly* taught me how to use polite words and expressions.

SECTION B   Used as an Adjective

In this usage the expression describes a degree of some quality and it can have either a positive or negative implication.

EXAMPLES

3. この   正月休み には そうとうな 道路混雑 が 予想 されます。
   Kono shōgatsu-yasumi ni wa   sōtō   na *dōro-konzatsu ga yosō   saremasu.*

   A *considerable* traffic jam is expected during the coming New Year holidays.

4. 今回 の 研究発表 で 彼女 は そうとう の 評価 を 得た。
   Konkai no kenkyū-happyō de kanojo wa   sōtō   *no hyōka o eta.*

   The paper she recently published has brought her into *fairly high* esteem in academic circles.

5. 十年間 も 勉強 している ので, 彼 の 日本語 は そうとう なもの
   Jūnen-kan mo benkyō shite iru node, kare no Nihongo wa   sōtō   na *mono*
   だ。
   da.

Having studied Japanese for the past ten years, his Japanese is *really* good. (It is the equivalent of ten years of study.)

6. 他人 の 考えをいかにも 自分自身 の 意見のようにして 言うと
   Tanin no kangae o   ikani mo jibun-jishin no iken no yō ni shite iu   to

   は, 彼 もそうとう な もの だ。
   wa, kare mo   sōtō   na *mono da.*

   He is the *kind* of person who uses other people's ideas as if they were his own. (He is that type of person.)

SECTION C Used to Indicate Equivalency

Used in this sense, the expression means something that is *equal to* or *appropriate to*.

EXAMPLES

7. この 競技に 優勝した 方には 十万円 に 相当する 賞品 が　贈
   Kono kyōgi ni yūshō shita kata ni wa jūman-en ni sōtō suru *shōhin ga oku-*

   られます。
   raremasu.

   The person who wins this contest will be given a prize *worth* one hundred thousand yen. (It will be equivalent in value to one hundred thousand yen.)

8. どんな 理由が あっても，人を殺した 罪 は死に相当する。
   Don'na riyū ga   atte mo, hito o koroshita tsumi wa shi ni sōtō suru.

   Regardless of the reasons involved, death is the only *appropriate* sentence for someone who commits the crime of murder.

Tada ただ   nothing but, only, once, gratis, free,
                   for nothing, ordinary, common, typical

EXPLANATION: The expression **tada** can be used in a wide variety of ways. More so than most of the other expressions discussed in this book, rather than conveying a precise or limited meaning or nuance, it often functions as an expression which gives an emphasis to the word or information which follows it. Although this usage is most clearly illustrated in Section F, it can be seen to some

degree in the other sections as well, though readers should be aware
of the specific meanings which **tada** can convey, as the various
examples below illustrate.

SECTION A Nothing But, Only

When used as shown below, **tada** refers to a singular action or
emotion, which is often translated as *nothing but* or *only*.

EXAMPLES

1. 病院 に 運ばれて から 今日 まで, 彼 は ただ 眠り続けて いる。
   Byōin ni hakobarete kara kyō made, kare wa tada *nemuri-tsuzukete iru.*

   From the time he was taken to the hospital until today, he's
   done *nothing but* sleep.

2. 私　　が理由をきいても, 妹 はただ泣くだけ だった。
   Watakushi ga riyū o   kiite mo, imōto wa tada *naku dake   datta.*

   I asked her why, but my sister *only* kept on crying.

3. ご親切　　にはただただ 感謝 しております。
   Go-shinsetsu ni wa tada tada *kansha shite orimasu.*

   I am *simply* very grateful for your kindness.

SECTION B Once, Only One

Tada can be used with numbers and counters. In its most common
usage, it is used in connection with the number one, to signify
something that is singular, that happened *only once*, or to refer to
a *single* individual. The usual counters in Japanese used with *tada*
are *ichido (once), ikkai (one time), hitotsu (one)* and *hitori (one
person)*, etc.

EXAMPLES

4. 田中氏　 にはただ 一度しか 会ったこと がありません。
   Tanaka-shi ni wa tada *ichido shika   atta   koto ga arimasen.*

   I have met Mr. Tanaka only *once*.

5. ただ 一度 の 誤り だけで その 人 を 評価する のは よくありま
   Tada ichido no ayamari dake de   sono hito o hyōka suru no wa yoku arima-
   せん。
   sen.

It is not fair to judge him by the *one* mistake he made.

6. 彼女　の 提案 に 賛成 したのは ただ 一人 だけ だった。
Kanojo no teian ni sansei shita no wa tada *hitori dake datta.*

There was *only one* person who agreed with her proposal.

SECTION C Free, Gratis

When used to refer to money or cost, the expression **tada** indicates something is *free* or *gratis* or *without charge*.

EXAMPLES

7. 将来 は スチュワーデス に なりたい と 思います。ただ で 世界旅行
Shōrai wa suchuwādesu   ni   naritai   to omoimasu. Tada *de sekai-ryokō*
が できますから。
ga dekimasu kara.

In the future I want to become an airline stewardess, because then I can see the world *for free*.

8. そんな に 高い 本 を 買う 必要 は ありません。図書館 に 行けば た
Son'na ni takai hon o kau hitsuyō wa arimasen.   Toshokan ni ikeba ta-
だ で 読める でしょう。
da *de yomeru deshō.*

There is no need to buy such an expensive book. You may read it *for free* at the library.

9. この シャツ が 千円 ですか，まるで ただ のよう ですね。
Kono shatsu ga sen-en desu ka,   marude tada *no yō desu ne.*

This shirt is one thousand yen! It's almost a *giveway*, isn't it?

SECTION D A Conclusion Leading to Consequence

When **tada** becomes part of the set expression **tada** *de sumu*, it means something that is finished resulting in an obligation or something which has come to an end and is now in a critical stage.

EXAMPLES

10. 人 の 車 に 傷をつけて，ただ ですむ と 思って いる のです
Hito no kuruma ni kizu o tsukete,   tada *de sumu to omotte iru no desu*
か。
ka.

You made a dent in someone's car. Do you think it's nothing serious?

11. このことが 社長に知れたら，ただではすまされないだろう。
    Kono koto ga shachō ni shiretara, tada de wa sumasarenai *darō.*

    Once the boss learns about this, something terrible will happen.

12. 私　　の不注意から皆さんに　ご迷惑　をかけて，ただです
    Watakushi no fuchūi kara minasan ni　go-meiwaku o　kakete, tada de su-
    むとは思っております。
    mu *to wa omotte　orimasen.*

    Because of my oversight I've caused all of you this trouble, and I'm fully aware of the obligation which I have to repay.

SECTION E Ordinary, Common

When the combination of **tada no** plus a noun is used, the idea is conveyed that something is *ordinary, typical* or *common,* as sentence No. 16 below shows. Used with a negative verb, as shown in sentences Nos. 13, 14 and 15, it indicates that something is *special, not common* or *not typical.*

EXAMPLES

13. これはただの風邪ではないようです。
    Kore wa tada no *kaze de wa nai　yō desu.*

    It seems this is no *ordinary* cold.

14. 七か国語　　も話せるとは，全く　ただの人ではない。
    Nanaka-kokugo mo hanaseru to wa, mattaku tada no *hito de wa nai.*

    I've heard he can speak seven languages. He is really a *special* person.

15. このやり方はただの　強盗殺人　ではありません。何か　個人的
    Kono yarikata wa tada no *gōtō-satsujin de wa arimasen. Nanika kojin-teki*
    な理由がありそうです。
    na riyū ga　arisō　desu.

    Because of the way it was committed, this is no *ordinary* homicide. It appears there was some personal motive involved.

16. 心配　ありません。ただの風邪ですから静かに寝ていればすぐ
    Shimpai arimasen.　Tada no *kaze desu kara shizuka ni nete　ireba　sugu*

直ります。
naorimasu.

There is no cause for worry. Since it's just an *ordinary* cold, some quiet bedrest will soon cure it.

SECTION F   But, Nevertheless, Provided

Tada is also used as a conjunction which indicates that the information following it in the sentence is to be emphasized as an exceptional remark to the immediately preceding statement. It is possible to translate it in a variety of ways, as the examples below illustrate.

EXAMPLES

17. あの店 のステーキはとてもうまい。ただ すこし 値段 が 高い が。
    Ano mise no   sutēki   wa totemo umai. Tada *sukoshi nedan ga takai ga.*
    That store's steak is really good, *but* the price is simply too high.

18. 彼 は有能な ビジネスマンです。ただ気の 短い のが 欠点 です。
    Kare wa yūnō na bijinesuman desu. Tada *ki no mijikai no ga ketten desu.*
    He is a competent businessman, *nevertheless* his weakness is a short temper.

19. 君 の案は 大変 面白い。 ただ 現実性 に乏しいのではない
    Kimi no an wa taihen omoshiroi. Tada *genjitsu-sei ni toboshii no de wa   nai*
    か。
    ka.
    Your proposal is very interesting, *but* there is really not much chance of putting it through, is there.

20. 彼 はとても 無口 だ。ただ 自分に 興味 のあることに 関して
    Kare wa totemo mukuchi da. Tada *jibun ni kyōmi no aru   koto ni kanshite*
    はよくしゃべる。
    wa yoku shaberu.
    He is very reticent, *nevertheless* he is very talkative when the subject arouses his interest.

21. 私 は 欠点 の多い人間です。ただけっしてうそを 言わな
    Watakushi wa ketten no   ōi ningen desu. Tada *kesshite uso o   iwana-*

いこと だけ は 信じて ください。
i   koto dake wa shinjite kudasai.

I am a person with a lot of faults, but *one thing for sure*, please believe me I never tell lies.

Taka ga たかが   only, merely, at most

EXPLANATION: The root of the expression **taka** refers to a volume or an amount. In colloquial usage, when referring to numbers or to action, it is used to stress the smallness of the numbers or the insignificance of the action. The final verb of the sentence need not be negative because **taka ga** always indicates that the specified numbers or action which follows it in the sentence is considered small or unimportant.

SECTION A   Only (Referring to Numbers)

When referring to numbers and amounts, the expression **taka ga** indicates that the numbers are few or the amount is low. It is similar to the Japanese expression *tatta (only)* (as illustrated in Section A of *Tatta*) except that **taka ga** is the stronger of the two expressions in emphasizing the smallness of the number, or the insignificance of the amount.

EXAMPLES

1. たか が 五千円 の 寄付 です。出せない はず は ない でしょう。
   Taka ga *gosen-en no kifu desu.   Dasenai hazu wa nai deshō.*

   It's *only* a five thousand yen donation. I don't see why you can't afford that much.

2. たか が 十キロ 歩いた だけ で こんな に 疲れて しまった。年 の せ
   Taka ga *jukkiro aruita dake de kon'na ni tsukarete shimatta. Toshi no se-*
   い か な。
   i   ka na.

   I've walked a *mere* ten kilometers and I'm this tired. Am I getting old?

3. たか が 一週間 の 旅行 に，そんな に たくさん 服 を 持って 行かな
Taka ga *isshūkan no ryokō ni,   son'na ni takusan fuku o   motte   ikana-*
くて も いい でしょう。
kute   mo   ii   deshō.

For *only* a week's vacation you don't have to take that many
clothes with you, do you?

SECTION B   Merely (Referring to Actions)
When some action or affair is considered very unimportant or very
insignificant, the expression **taka ga** is used as shown below.

EXAMPLES

4. たか が 盲腸 の 手術 です。心配 する こと は ありません。
Taka ga *mōchō no shujutsu desu. Shimpai suru koto wa   arimasen.*

It's *only* an appendectomy, so there is no need to worry.

5. たか が 子ども の けんか に， 親 が 出て いく という の は まったく
Taka ga *kodomo no kenka ni,   oya ga dete iku to iu   no wa mattaku*
おかしい。
okashii.

It's *just* an argument between children, and there is absolutely
no reason for the parents to get involved.

6. たか が 風邪 だ など と 軽く みて は いけません。早く うち に 帰っ
Taka ga *kaze da nado to karuku mite wa ikemasen.   Hayaku uchi ni kaet-*
て お休み なさい。
te o-yasumi nasai.

It's wrong to say it's *only* a cold and treat it lightly. Hurry
home and get some rest.

Tashika   たしか   certainly, definitely, reliable, proper,
              (確か)   if I am correct, I think

EXPLANATION: The basic meaning of the expression **tashika**, as
shown in Sections A and B, refer to something that is *certain,
positive, trustworthy* and *reliable*. Popular conversational usages are
shown in Sections C and D, where it means *truly, for sure* (Section

C), or *I think, I suppose* (Section D). Note that the expression, though often used as it stands by being merely inserted into a sentence, takes the particle *na* when it modifies a noun (and acts as an adjective), and it takes the particle *ni* when it modifies a verb (and acts as an adverb).

SECTION A   Certain, Positive

This section illustrates the basic meaning of the expression **tashika**, which is similar to the Japanese expression *hontō da* (*for sure, for certain*). Used in this way, the expression refers to a stated proposition and confirms it.

EXAMPLES

1. 彼　が 今度 の 選挙 に 立候補する こと は，ほとんど たしか だ。
    Kare ga kondo no senkyo ni rikkōho suru koto wa,   hotondo tashika *da.*
    It's almost *certain* that he will run in this election.

2. 今日 は たしか な お返事 を 聞かせて ください。
    Kyō wa tashika *na o-henji o   kikasete kudasai.*
    Please give me a *definite* answer today.

3. 松本氏　　　の 理事長 就任 は たしか に なった。
    Matsumoto-shi no rijichō shūnin wa tashika *ni natta.*
    Mr. Matsumoto's appointment as director of the board has become *certain.*

4. あの うわさ は いよいよ たしか だ と 分った。
    Ano uwasa wa iyo-iyo tashika da to wakatta.
    That rumor has finally been proved to be *true.*

SECTION B   Reliable, Genuine

This section illustrates how **tashika** evaluates and confirms the positive character of the subject of the sentence. It is here similar in feeling to the Japanese expressions *tadashii* (*correct, proper*), and *machigai nai* (*without question*). Its usage in this manner still preserves its basic meaning as given in Section A above.

EXAMPLES

5. 彼　の 日本語 は たしか です。
   Kare no Nihongo wa tashika *desu.*

   His Japanese is quite *correct.*

6. あの 会社 は たしか だから，すぐ 契約 しても 大丈夫 です。
   Ano kaisha wa tashika *da kara,　sugu keiyaku shite mo daijōbu desu.*

   Since that company is *trustworthy,* it's okey to go ahead and sign a contract with them.

7. 私　　　の 母 はもう 九十歳 になりますが，まだ目も　耳も
   Watakushi no haha wa　mō kyūjussai ni narimasu ga, mada me mo mimi mo
   たしか です。
   tashika *desu.*

   Although my mother is already ninety, her eyes and ears are still *good.*

8. この ニュースはたしか な　所 から聞いた　話 です。
   Kono nyūsu　wa tashika *na tokoro kara kiita hanashi desu.*

   This news was given by a *reliable* source.

SECTION C　Truly, For Sure

In a very popular conversational usage, the expression **tashika**, as illustrated below, is similar to the Japanese expression *hontō ni* (*really, absolutely*) and *machigai naku (for sure*).

EXAMPLES

9. おつりを もらって たしか に この ポケット に いれた のに　なくなっ
   O-tsuri o moratte tashika ni *kono poketto ni ireta noni nakunat-*
   ている。
   te iru.

   I got the change and *definitely* put it in this pocket, but it's disappeared.

10. 家 を 出る 時 たしか に ドアにかぎを 掛けた のに，帰って みたら
    Uchi o deru toki tashika ni *doa ni kagi o kaketa noni, kaette mitara*
    開いて いた。
    aite ita.

Although when leaving the house I *definitely* locked the door, when I returned I found it was open.

11. 先週　たしかに　速達 を出した のに,　彼 は まだ受け取ってい
    Senshū tashika ni *sokutatsu o　dashita noni,　kare wa mada　uketotte　i-*
ない と 言う。
nai　to　u.

Although I *absolutely* sent that letter by special delivery last week, he says he hasn't received it yet.

SECTION D   Probably, I Suppose

A further popular conversational usage of **tashika** carries meanings similar to the Japanese expression *tabun (probably, most likely)*. It indicates a slight uncertainty on the part of the speaker about the accuracy of the statement, but it also implies that the statement is *probably* accurate.

EXAMPLES

12. 彼　に 会った の は たしか　先週 の 金曜日 です。
    Kare ni　atta　no wa tashika *senshū no kin'yōbi desu.*

I'm *almost certain* it was last Friday when I met him.

13. この 時計 は たしか　三万円 だった と 思います。
    Kono tokei wa tashika *samman-en datta　to omoimasu.*

If I *remember correctly* this watch cost thirty thousand yen.

14. たしか この 辺 に ポスト が あった と 思う の だが, どうしても 見
    Tashika *kono hen ni posuto ga　atta　to omou no da ga,　dōshite mo mi-*
つからない。
tsukaranai.

I *thought* there was a mailbox around here, but I can't seem to find it.

Tatta たった   only, just, merely

EXPLANATION: **Tatta** is used to refer to something that is of a very small quantity or of a very short duration. Thus it always emphasizes the smallness of the number or time to which it refers. In modern American English, the three possible translations shown above are interchangeable in many instances, although in the examples below the most natural sounding translations have been given.

SECTION A Only (Referring to Numbers)

When used in reference to numbers, the expression **tatta** means *only* or *merely* and indicates that the number is not considered to be large.

EXAMPLES

1. 一生懸命 に 節約 したけれども, 貯金 はたった 五十万円 し
   Isshōkemmei ni setsuyaku shita keredomo, chokin wa tatta *gojūman-en shi-*
   かない。
   ka nai.

   I tried hard to be frugal, but I *only* have five hundred thousand yen in savings.

2. たった 三百頁 の 本を読むのに, 一週間 も かかってしまっ
   Tatta *sambyaku-peiji no hon o yomu no ni, isshūkan mo kakatte shimat-*
   た。
   ta.

   Although the book I read had *only* three hundred pages, it took me a week to read it.

3. 彼等 はたった 一度 会っただけで 結婚 の 約束 をしたそう
   Karera wa tatta *ichido atta dake de kekkon no yakusoku o shita sō*
   だ。
   da.

   Although they've met *only* once, I've heard that they are engaged.

SECTION B Just (Referring to Time)

When referring to time, **tatta** means something that has *just now* happened; it indicates that very little or almost no time has passed since the action in question. In common speech, it is often used as part of the expression **tatta ima** (*just now*).

EXAMPLES

4. 主人 はたった今出掛けた ところ です。
   Shūjin wa tatta ima *dekaketa tokoro desu.*

   My husband has *just* gone out.

5. 「おそくなって すみません。 ずいぶん お待ちに なりましたか。」
   "Osokunatte   sumimasen.   Zuibun   o-machi ni narimashita ka?"

   「いいえ， たった今来た ばかり です。」
   "Iie,   tatta ima kita bakari desu."

   "Sorry I'm late. Have you waited very long?"
   "No, I've *just* gotten here."

6. たった今 話した こと を もう 忘れてしまった の ですか。
   Tatta ima *hanashita koto o   mō wasurete shimatta no desu ka?*

   Have you already forgotten what I've *just* told you?

Tokaku   とかく   frequently, often, repeatedly, tend to, be apt to

EXPLANATION: The expression **tokaku** always carries with it a feeling of something that is *frequent* or *repeated*, as opposed to anything that is singular or unique. Therefore it is used to refer to multiple reasons or repeated actions.

SECTION A Repeated or Frequent Actions
Tokaku, in this usage, is similar to the Japanese expression *shibashiba*, which means *often, frequently* or *repeatedly*. It gives a sense of frequent and continuing action.

EXAMPLES

1. 利己主義 と 個人主義 は とかく 混同 されやすい。
   Riko-shugi to kojin-shugi wa tokaku *kondō sare-yasui.*

   The meaning of the terms "egoism" and "individualism" are *often* easily confused.

2. 仲 が よすぎる と とかく けんか する もの です。
   Naka ga yosugiru to tokaku *kenka suru mono desu.*

Being too close to someone is *frequently* a cause of arguments.

3. 仕事　の速い　人　は　とかく　失敗　も　多い　もの です。
   Shigoto no hayai hito wa tokaku *shippai mo ōi   mono desu.*

   People who work quickly *often* make many mistakes.

SECTION B   Multiple Reasons

To indicate that there are *several, many* and *various* factors involved in some situation, **tokaku** can be used as illustrated below. Its meaning here is similar to the Japanese expression *iro-iro* (*various, several*).

EXAMPLES

4. あの 人 は とかく うわさ が ある 人 ですから，　気 を つけた ほう が
   Ano hito wa tokaku *uwasa ga aru hito desu kara,   ki o tsuketa hō ga*
   いい です よ。
   ii   desu yo.

   There is *all kind* of gossip about that person, so you'd better be careful.

5. とかく する うち に，帰国 の 時期 が 迫って きた。
   Tokaku *suru uchi ni, kikoku no jiki ga sematte kita.*

   While being busy with *various* things, the time to return home approached.

6. とかく この 世 は 住みにくい，　いっそ 山 の 中 に 入って ひとり
   Tokaku *kono yo wa suminikui,   isso yama no naka ni haitte   hitori*
   で 暮そう か。
   de kurasō ka.

   Considering everything it's so hard to live in this world; should I go into the mountains and live alone? (Note that the first portion of this sentence, *"kono yo wa suminikui"* (*it's so hard to live in this world*), is considered a truism and is used as a set phrase or as a colloquial saying in Japanese. The remainder of a sentence used with this phrase can express whatever additional comment or followup idea the speaker wishes to make. Used in this way, *tokaku* carries a sense of fatalism with it, conveying the idea that in this life there are many difficult problems that simply cannot be avoided.)

Tonikaku   とにかく

first of all, first, before that,
especially, most of all, anyway,
anyhow, at any rate

EXPLANATION: **Tonikaku** is an expression which carries a feeling
that an action or idea or situation expressed in the portion of the
sentence following **tonikaku,** must take priority over whatever was
said in the first part of the sentence. As shown in Section A, it
means something that should be done or considered *first,* or *before
anything else.* Or, as shown in Section B, it refers to something that
was extreme or which had predominance over whatever else was
expressed in the sentence. It can also be used by itself as a single
word sentence, to mean something like, " well, *first of all....*"

SECTION A First of All

When used in regard to actions, **tonikaku** refers to an action which
the speaker wishes to perform *before* performing any other actions.
Thus it can easily be translated as *first of all* or *before that.*

EXAMPLES

1. いろいろ 言いたい こと も ある だろうが, とにかく 私 の
   Iro-iro   iitai   koto mo aru   darō ga,   tonikaku watakushi no
   話 を 聞きなさい。
   hanashi o   kikinasai.

   There are probably many things you want to say, but *first* please
   listen to what I have to say.

2. 一杯やりたいけれど, とにかく 仕事 を 片付けてしまおう。
   Ippai yaritai   keredo,   tonikaku shigoto o katazukete shimaō.

   I just want to have a drink, but I'd better finish my work *first.*

3. 考えている だけ では なに も できない, とにかく やってみよう。
   Kangaete iru dake de wa nani mo dekinai,   tonikaku yatte miyō.

   It won't do any good to just think about it, so let's try and see
   anyway.

SECTION B Especially

Tonikaku can also be used to refer to a situation that is considered extreme or to some situation that is of most concern. For example, it can refer to weather that was *so* cold (extremely cold). Its use is shown below.

EXAMPLES

4. 久し振り に 日本 に 帰って 来た が, とにかく 物価 が 高い のに は
    Hisashiburi ni Nihon ni kaette kita ga, tonikaku *bukka ga takai no ni wa*
    驚いた。
    odoroita.

    After a long while away I returned to Japan, and I was astonished that prices had gotten *so* high.

5. おそく なって すみません, とにかく 道 がこんでいて どうにも
    Osoku   natte   sumimasen, tonikaku *michi ga konde ite   dō   ni mo*
    なりません でした。
    narimasen   deshita.

    I'm sorry to be late, but since the traffic was *especially* heavy there was nothing I could do.

6. 知床岬   まで行きましたが, とにかく 寒くて 景色 を 楽
    Shiretoko-misaki made ikimashita ga, tonikaku *samukute keshiki o tano-*
    しむ こと など できません でした。
    shimu koto nado dekimasen   deshita.

    I went as far as Shiretoko-misaki, but since it was *so* cold I couldn't enjoy the scenery. (Note that Shiretoko-misaki is in the northeastern part of Japan's northern island of Hokkaido.)

Tōtei とうてい   (cannot) possibly, absolutely (not),
    （到底）   (not) at all

EXPLANATION: The expression **tōtei** means something which has reached the bottom, or when used conversationally, it refers to the "bottom line" of a situation. It is always used to express a negative situation, to give the feeling that something is *not at all possible* or *absolutely cannot* be done. It is sometimes used as a shortcut expression to indicate a negative situation, but without stating the reasoning, as illustrated in sentence No. 4.

EXAMPLES

1. あの 正直 な 彼 が, 人 を だます と は, とうてい 信じられない こ
   Ano shōjiki na kare ga,   hito o damasu to wa,   tōtei   shinjirarenai ko-
   と だ。
   to da.

   I *cannot possibly* believe that he who is so honest would cheat anyone.

2. 両親　は 東大 へ 行け と 言う けれども,　　私　　の　　能力 では
   Ryōshin wa Tōdai e ike to iu   keredomo, watakushi no nōryoku de wa
   とうてい 無理 だ。
   tōtei   muri da.

   My parents told me to enter the University of Tokyo, but I'm *not at all* good enough to do it. (I don't have the ability to do it.)

3. 今年　　上半期　に 景気 が 好転する こと は, とうてい 期待 できな
   Kotoshi kami-hanki ni keiki ga kōten suru koto wa,   tōtei   kitai dekina-
   い。
   i.

   I have *absolutely no* hope that business conditions will improve during the first half of the year.

4. この 雨 では, とうてい タクシー は つかまらない だろう。
   Kono ame de wa,   tōtei   takushii wa tsukamaranai darō.

   With this rain, *won't it be hard* to catch a taxi. (Implying that everyone will be taking taxis to avoid the rain.)

Totemo　とても　doesn't at all, cannot possibly, never, very, quite, extremely

EXPLANATION: The expression **totemo** is always used to refer to some extreme condition. As shown in Section A, it is used to modify a negative verb and means *cannot possibly* or *not at all*. When used to modify an adjective, a popular usage shown illustrated in Section B, is means something that is *very* or *extremely* something.

SECTION A   Cannot Possibly

When used to modify a verb which is negative, **totemo** indicates a feeling of *cannot possibly*. This usage is similar to the expression *tōtei* which is discussed elsewhere in this book.

EXAMPLES

1. 山下夫人　　　はいつも 若若しくて，　　大学生 の 息子 の 母
   Yamashita-fujin wa itsumo wakawakashikute, daigakusei no musuko no haha
   にはとても見えない。
   ni wa totemo *mienai.*

   Mrs. Yamashita always seems so young, she *doesn't at all* look like a mother who has a son in college.

2. 仕事　 の ために 自分 を 売る こと など，　　私　 にはとても でき
   Shigoto no tame ni jibun o   uru   koto nado, watakushi ni wa totemo *deki-*
   ません。
   masen.

   I *cannot possibly* sell myself just for the sake of a job.

3. この 眠ったように 静か な 村 に 血生臭い　争い が 起った と
   Kono nemutta yō ni shizuka na mura ni chinamagusai arasoi ga okotta   to
   は，とても信じられない。
   wa, totemo *shinjirarenai.*

   It's *hard* to believe that such a bloody battle could have taken place in this sleepy, quiet village.

SECTION B   Very, Quite

In its most popular usage, the expression **totemo** is used to modify an adjective, and its nuance is one of indicating an extreme condition, such as *very* much, *quite* a lot, etc. It is similar in feeling to the popular Japanese expression *taihen* (*very, quite*).

EXAMPLES

4. この お菓子 は とても おいしい です よ。
   Kono okashi wa totemo   *oishii   desu yo.*

   This candy is *very* good.

5. あの 方 はとてもいい 人です。
   Ano kata wa totemo   *ii   hito desu.*

That is a *very* fine person.

6. 今日 は とても 楽しかった。
   Kyō wa totemo *tanoshikatta.*

   I was *very* happy today.

Tōtō とうとう   finally, at last, in the end

EXPLANATION: The expression **tōtō** always refers to some long process that has finally reached a conclusion. It is almost exactly the same in its nuances and possible uses as the Japanese expression *tsui ni* (*at last, after all*). *Tsui ni* is discussed elsewhere in this book and that section should be especially compared with the uses of **tōtō** as given in this section. Please note that the expression **tōtō** is most commonly used in conversational speech. It is somewhat similar to the Japanese expression *kekkyoku* (*consequently*) as it is discussed elsewhere in this book; see *kekkyoku*, Section A. However, as it is discussed below in Section C, examples 5 and 6, simply the fact of the result is noted (not the idea that there has been a process leading up to the result). In the usage discussed below it refers merely to the outcome of something and might be translated as *in the end*.

SECTION A Positive Implication

Tōtō can be used, as illustrated below, to indicate that a long expected or long desired result has finally been achieved.

EXAMPLES

1. 十年 以上 かかった 研究 が とうとう 完成 した。
   Jū-nen ijō   kakatta kenkyū ga   totō   kansei shita.

   The research that has taken me more than ten years to do has *finally* been completed.

2. 長かった 学生生活 が 終り，社会人 として 出発 する 日
   Nagakatta gakusei-seikatsu ga owari, shakai-jin to shite shuppatsu suru hi

が とうとう 来た。

ga tōtō *kita.*

My long period as a student is finished, and the time to go out into the world has *at last* come.

SECTION B Negative Implication

Tōtō can also be used with a negative implication, to convey the feeling that the final result of a situation has confirmed the speaker's fears.

EXAMPLES

3. 十年　近く飼っていた愛犬が とうとう 死んでしまった。
Jū-nen chikaku katte ita aiken ga tōtō *shinde shimatta.*
The pet dog I kept for nearly ten years died *at last.*

4. 最後 の お金 も とうとう 使い果たしてしまった。
Saigo no o-kane mo tōtō *tsukai hatashite shimatta.*
In the end I even used up my last bit of money.

SECTION C Unexpected Outcome

The expression **tōtō** also refers to a final result or an outcome which has taken place. It is used usually with a negative verb, in which case it indicates that the final result turned out differently than had been expected by the speaker. That is to say, it was an unexpected outcome.

EXAMPLES

5. 忙しくて あの 展覧会には とうとう 行けませんでした。
Isogashikute ano tenrankai ni wa tōtō *ikemasen deshita.*
Being busy, I was *in the end* unable to go to that exhibition.

6. 一時間 も 待ったが 彼女 は, とうとう 現われなかった。
Ichi-jikan mo matta ga, kanojo wa tōtō *arawarenakatta.*
I waited at least an hour but she *never* appeared.

Tsui つい   just, only, unthinkingly, unintentionally, carelessly

EXPLANATION: In what is perhaps its most common usage, the expression **tsui** gives a sense of closeness or proximity in regard to an action, and it refers to something that *has just* happened, as illustrated in Section A. Its implication when referring to a location, as illustrated in Section B, is similar. These two usages tend to be close in concept, while its use as illustrated in Section C is quite different, since it can also be used to indicate an action that is *carelessly, unintentionally* or *accidentially* done.   The third usage is not so different from a purely logical point of view, because it gives a sense of something being so close to the speaker that it was overlooked.

SECTION A   Just Now

To indicate an extremely short, almost immediate time period, the expression is used as illustrated below. It means something *has just* happened, or was *just* happening, or was *just about to* happen.

EXAMPLES

1. 吉田さん　にはついこの　二,三日　前 に 会いました。
   Yoshida-san ni wa tsui *kono ni-san-nichi mae ni   aimashita.*

   I met Mr. Yoshida *just* two or three days ago.

2. 彼　はつい さっきまでいたの ですが，もう 帰りました。
   Kare wa tsui   *sakki   made   ita   no desu ga,   mō   kaerimashita.*

   He was here until *just* a short while ago, but he has gone home now.

3. 三年　　前 のあの日 が，　つい きのうのことのように 思い出さ
   San-nen mae no ano hi ga,   tsui   *kinō   no koto no yō   ni omoi dasa-*
   れる。
   reru.

   I can remember that day three years ago as if it were *only* yesterday.

SECTION B   Nearby

When used with reference to a place or location, **tsui** implies that the object of the sentence is very near. Its actual translation when used in this manner would be *just* or *only*, as shown below. In this section **tsui** always refers to a physical location.

EXAMPLES

4. 駅 はここからつい　　二,三百米　　先 です。
   Eki wa koko kara tsui ni-sambyaku-mētoru saki desu.
   The station is *only* two or three hundred meters ahead.

5. お互 につい 近く に住んでいる のに, めったに 会いません。
   Otagai ni tsui chikaku ni sunde iru noni, metta ni aimasen.
   Although we live *quite* nearby, we rarely meet.

6. 家内 はついそこまで　買物 に出掛けた の ですから,　すぐ帰っ
   Kanai wa tsui soko made kaimono ni dekaketa no desu kara, sugu kaet-
   て来る でしょう。
   te kuru deshō.
   Since my wife went *just* over there to buy something, she should be coming back soon.

SECTION C   Carelessly, Unintentionally

When referring to something that was the result of *carelessness*, **tsui** is used as illustrated below. Its meaning in this usage is similar to the Japanese expression *omowazu* (*in spite of myself*) and *ukkari* (*absent-mindedly*), both of which are discussed elsewhere in this book.

EXAMPLES

7. たばこ を止めよう と思う の ですが,　人 が 吸っている と つい 吸
   Tabako o yameyō to omou no desu ga, hito ga sutte iru to tsui su-
   ってしまいます。
   tte shimaimasu.
   I intend to stop smoking, but when others are smoking I *un-thinkingly* smoke.

8. 話　　に 夢中になって,　時間 が たつの をつい 忘れてしまった。
   Hanashi ni muchū ni natte, jikan ga tatsu no o tsui wasurete shimatta.

Since I was so absorbed in talking, I *unexpectedly* lost track of the time.

9. 「めくら」,「つんぼ」,「おし」 などは　差別語 だ と 知って は います
   "Mekura," "tsumbo," "oshi"　nado wa sabetsu-go da to　shitte wa imasu
   が, 慣用句 の　中　ではつい 使ってしまいます。
   ga, kan'yō-ku no naka de wa tsui tsukatte shimaimasu.

I know the words "mekura" (to be blind), "tsumbo" (to be deaf) and "oshi" (to be mute) should not be used, but I often *carelessly* use them in conversation. (Note that these three words are not proper medical terms but are slang and carry a pejorative connotation. By unwritten convention they are never used in radio broadcasting or in the mass media.)

Tsuide ni　ついでに　　while, in passing,
　　　　　　　　　　　　if you have the occasion to

EXPLANATION:　When used between two phrases or sentences, this expression refers to a secondary or related action which can be performed in the course of carrying out the major action of the sentence. It is used in the sense of "while I am doing A, why don't I also do B". The action referred to in the clause following **tsuide ni** can be considered to express the subordinate action of the sentence.

EXAMPLES

1. 丸善　に 来た ついでに ちょっと 近く の　高島屋　に も　寄って
   Maruzen ni kita tsuide ni *chotto chikaku no Takashimaya ni mo　yotte*
   みよう。
   miyō.

   Since I'm going to Maruzen, I'll stop at nearby Takashimaya too. (The subject of this sentence, since it is not clearly stated, can also be plural in this case: *Since* we're going to Maruzen, let's stop at Takashimaya too.)

2. 買物　に 行く の なら, ついでに この 手紙　も 出して 来て くださ
   Kaimono ni iku no nara, tsuide ni *kono tegami mo dashite kite kudasa-*

いませんか。
imasen ka?

While you're going out shopping, won't you mail this letter for me?

Tsui ni ついに   in the end, finally, at last, after all
（遂に）

EXPLANATION: **Tsui ni** gives the feeling that a long on-going process has finally come to an end and the results of that process can now be seen. It can be used in a positive or negative sense, but always with the idea that the outcome seems quite clear. Sections A, B and C below are similar in usage and meaning to the expression *tōtō*, Sections A, B and C, as it is discussed elsewhere in this book.

SECTION A Positive Implication
Used in this sense, the expression indicates that the achieved results are according to the speaker's wishes or hopes.

EXAMPLES

1. 何度 も 失敗を 重ねたが，ついに 実験に成功した。
   Nando mo shippai o kasaneta ga, tsui ni *jikken ni seikō shita.*

   I made many mistakes, but *in the end* I completed the experiment.

2. 長い 間 独身 を 続けていた彼女も，ついにこの春 結婚 す
   Nagai aida dokushin o tsuzukete ita kanojo mo, tsui ni *kono haru kekkon su-*
   るらしい。
   ru rashii.

   It looks like even she, who has long been living alone, will *finally* be getting married this spring.

SECTION B Negative Implication
In this case, **tsui ni** means that the outcome of a situation simply confirmed the speaker's fears or worries, and the expression conveys a negative implication.

EXAMPLES

3. あんなに丈夫だった彼も，重い病気にかかり ついに 死んでしま
   An'na ni jōbu datta kare mo, omoi byōki ni kakari tsui ni *shinde shima-*
   った。
   tta.

   Even he who was always so healthy, became seriously ill and
   in the end died.

4. 大事に使っていた　退職金 も ついになくなってしまった。
   Daiji ni tsukatte ita taishoku-kin mo tsui ni *nakunatte shimatta.*

   Even the retirement fund, which was always used carefully, was
   at last used up.

SECTION C Unexpected Outcome

Occasionally **tsui ni** is also used to indicate an outcome that was
contrary to the expected outcome.

EXAMPLES

5. 何度 も 電話したのに，友だち はついに 出なかった。
   Nando mo denwa shita no ni, tomodachi wa tsui ni *denakatta.*

   Although I telephoned several times, my friend *never* answered
   the phone.

6. 多くの　力自慢　の 人々 が 挑戦したが，ついに 彼 には 勝
   Ōku no chikara-jiman no hitobito ga chōsen shita ga, tsui ni *kare ni wa ka-*
   てなかった。
   tenakatta.

   Many strong and boastful people have challenged him, but *in
   the end* no one could beat him.

Tsuku-zuku　つくづく　　　　thoroughly, entirely, sadly,
regretfully, stare intently,
gaze earnestly

EXPLANATION: This expression comes from the verb *tsukiru*, which
means to be *used up*, to be *consumed* or *to run out of* something.
Thus it can be conversationally applied in a number of ways to

refer to human actions. Section A describes something that is *thoroughly* considered, Section B something that is *greatly missed*, and Section C illustrates how it describes a gaze that is *earnest* or *intent*.

SECTION A To Consider Thoroughly, Deeply, Fully

As illustrated below, **tsuku-zuku** can be used to refer to something that has been pondered or considered *thoroughly* or which has been thought through *fully*.

EXAMPLES

1. つくづく　考えると，やっぱり老後は不安です。
   Tsuku-zuku *kangaeru to,　yappari　rōgo wa fuan desu.*
   When I *really* think about it, I feel old age is filled with anxiety.

2. きのうの夜 つくづく と 考えて みましたが，　この　仕事 は
   Kinō　no yoru tsuku-zuku *to　kangaete mimashita ga,　kono　shigoto wa*
   私　　に向かないと思います。
   watakushi ni　mukanai　to omoimasu.
   I considered it very *thoroughly* last night, and this work just doesn't suit me.

SECTION B To Lament, To Long For

In contrast to Section A, when the expression **tsuku-zuku** is used in a more-or-less objective sense, as shown below, it carries an emotional feeling, one of *longing for*, or *lamenting*, or *grieving for* or *missing very much*. A feeling of *remorse* can also be implied.

EXAMPLES

3. 今度 のことで 自分には才能がないとつくづく　思い知った。
   Kondo no koto de, jibun ni wa sainō ga　nai　to tsuku-zuku *omoi-shitta.*
   This time I've *sadly* come to realize that I have no talent.

4. 何　も思うようにならない世の中がつくづくいやになりま
   Nani mo omou　yō　ni　naranai yo no naka ga tsuku-zuku *iya　ni narima-*
   した。
   shita.

I'm *sick of* this world in which nothing goes the way I want it to.

5. つくづく　思い出されるのは死んだ息子のやさしさです。
Tsuku-zuku omoi-dasareru no wa shinda musuko no yasashisa desu.

What *grieves* me most is to recall how sweet my dead son was.

SECTION C To Gaze Earnestly

When a stare or gaze is *deep* or *penetrating*, the opposite of a quick or casual glance, **tsuku-zuku** is used as illustrated below.

EXAMPLES

6. 老人は　私　の顔をつくづくと見て,「お母様とそっくりだ」
Rōjin wa watakushi no kao o tsuku-zuku *to mite, "Okāsama to　sokkuri da"*
とつぶやいた。
to　tsubuyaita.

The old man looked *intently* at my face, then mumbled, "You look just like your mother."

7. 病人　はやせ細った自分の手をつくづくと眺めていた。
Byōnin wa yasehosotta jibun no te o tsuku-zuku *to nagamete ita.*

The patient stared *intently* at his thin hand.

8. 茶道具屋の主人はその茶碗をつくづくと見ていたが,「間
Chadōgu-ya no shujin wa sono chawan o tsuku-zuku *to mite ita ga, "Ma-*
違いありません, 本物の古伊万里です」と言った。
chigai arimasen, hommono no koimari　desu" to　itta.

The proprietor of the tea ceremony shop gazed *earnestly* at the tea bowl, then said, "No question, this is a real koimari-bowl."

Tsumari つまり in short, after all, in the end, in other words, in brief

EXPLANATION: The expression **tsumari** indicates some idea or piece of information that is being stated concisely, is being summed up, or is being restated by the speaker. It signals that the results of the topic under discussion are about to be stated, or restated.

SECTION A   To State Briefly

To indicate that some conclusion to a topic will be summed up or stated concisely, the expression is used as illustrated below.

EXAMPLES

1. はっきり言ってください, つまり病気は直らないのですね。
   Hakkiri   itte   kudasai, tsumari *byōki wa naoranai no desu ne.*

   Please speak plainly. This sickness, *in short,* cannot be cured, is that correct?

2. あなたの　話　はよく分りませんが, つまり　何　が言いたいの
   Anata   no hanashi wa yoku wakarimasen ga, tsumari *nani ga   iitai   no*

   ですか。
   desu ka?

   I can't understand what you are saying. What, *after all,* do you want to say?

3. 理由はいろいろあげられるが, つまり　予算が足りないというこ
   Riyū wa   iro-iro   agerareru ga, tsumari *yosan ga   tarinai   to   iu   ko-*

   とだ。
   to da.

   All sorts of reasons can be given, but *in the end* the real reason is that there is not enough money in the budget.

SECTION B   To Restate

Often, in both English and Japanese, when a conclusion to some topic has been stated, it is immediately restated, usually in a slightly more succinct manner. This usage of **tsumari** might be translated as *in other words.*

EXAMPLES

4. この　間　なくなったのが　父　の　母　の　妹,　つまり　　　　私
   Kono aida   nakunatta no ga   chichi no haha no imōto, tsumari *watakushi*

   の大おばです。
   no ōoba desu.

   The person who died recently was my father's mother's sister, or *in other words,* my great aunt.

5. マンション とか コーポ とか ハイム とか いう のは, つまり 高層住
   Manshon   toka kōpo   toka haimu toka   iu   no wa, tsumari *kōsōjū-*
   宅 の こと です。
   taku no koto desu.

   Words like mansion, co-op and heim mean, *in other words,* high-
   rise apartments.

6. 子ども を 家庭で どの ように 導き しつける べき か の 問題,
   Kodomo o   katei de dono yō ni michibiki shitsukeru beki ka no mondai,
   つまり 家庭教育 の 問題 について お話 したい と 思います。
   tsumari *katei-kyōiku no mondai ni tsuite o-hanashi shitai to omoimasu.*

   What I'd like to talk about is how families should give guidance
   to their children, or *in other words,* the question of discipline in
   the home.

Ukkari   うっかり   thoughtlessly, absent mindedly, carelessly

EXPLANATION: The expression **ukkari** refers to something that
was done without thinking (*thoughtlessly*) or which was done without having taken the necessary precautions (*carelessly*) It therefore
also refers to something done *absent mindedly* or *by mistake.* Section
A shows how it is used as an adverb and Section B gives examples
of the expression as a verb.

SECTION A Thoughtlessly, Absent-Mindedly

In the examples below, **ukkari** is used by itself and is simply inserted into the sentence, to indicate something that was done *carelessly* or *without thinking.* When used in this manner, **ukkari** is
similar to the expression *tsui* as discussed in this book under *Tsui,*
Section C, where it refers to an unexpected outcome.

EXAMPLES

1. 話して はいけない と 言われて いた のに, うっかり しゃべって し
   Hanashite wa ikenai to iwarete ita noni,   ukkari   *shabette shi-*
   まった。
   matta.

Although I was told not to mention it, I *thoughtlessly* told everything.

2. 電車　が　　品川駅　に止ったのに，考えごとをしていてうっか
   Densha ga Shinagawa-eki ni tomatta noni, kangae-goto o shite ite ukka-
   り乗り過ごしてしまった。
   ri *nori-sugoshite shimatta.*

   Although the train stopped at Shinagawa Station, while thinking about something I *absent-mindedly* rode the train past the station.

3. 教室　　では日本語以外話してはいけないと言われていたの
   Kyōshitsu de wa Nihongo igai hanashite wa ikenai to iwarete ita no-
   に，うっかり英語を使ってしまった。
   ni, ukkari *Eigo o tsukatte shimatta.*

   Although I had been told to only use Japanese in the classroom, I *absent-mindedly* used English.

SECTION B Absent-Mindedly, Carelessly

The meaning of **ukkari** as given below is essentially the same as that shown in Section A above. The difference is that below the expression becomes a verb, **ukkari** *suru*, which means to *do something thoughtlessly*, or to *do something carelessly*. One form which this expression often takes in popular usage is **ukkari** *shite iru to* (*if you do something carelessly . . .*).

EXAMPLES

4. この　道　は　車　が多いですから，うっかりしていると危険
   Kono michi wa kuruma ga ōi desu kara, ukkari shite iru to *kiken*
   ですよ。
   desu yo.

   Since there is a lot of traffic on the road, it's dangerous *if you're not careful.*

5. 最近　はよく眠れて，うっかりしていると朝寝過ごしてしまう。
   Saikin wa yoku nemurete, ukkari shite iru to *asa ne-sugoshite shimau.*

   I've been sleeping so well lately that *if I'm not careful* I'll oversleep.

6. うっかり して 手紙 に 切手 を はらないで ポスト に 入れて しまっ
   Ukkari   shite *tegami ni*   *kitte o haranaide*   *posuto ni irete shimat-*
   た。
   ta.

   I *absent-mindedly* put the letter in the mailbox without a stamp.

Waza-waza   わざわざ   take the trouble to, especially,
                                      on purpose, deliberately, knowingly

EXPLANATION: This expression is usually inserted directly in front
of the verb or verb phrase, and it does not take any particles. It
can appear in both positive and negative statements, although it
usually refers to a slightly negative circumstance. In most common
usage, it refers to a negative or unpleasant situation.

SECTION A   Polite / Positive Usage
In cases where the expression is used in a positive sense, it is usually
a polite way of acknowledging that someone has done something
troublesome as a courtesy to the speaker.

EXAMPLES
   1. わざわざ いらっしゃって くださって 本当 に ありがとう ございます。
      Waza-waza *irasshatte   kudasatte hontō ni   arigatō   gozaimasu.*

      I am really very grateful that you *took the trouble* to come here
      today.

   2. お忙しい ところ，わざわざ お返事 を くださって ありがとう ござい
      O-isogashii tokoro, waza-waza *o-henji o   kudasatte   arigatō   gozai-*
      ます。
      masu.

      I know you are busy, so I'm grateful you *were able* to reply.

SECTION B   Negative Implication, Because of Circumstances
Used in this sense, the expression indicates something which happened that was unexpected or not desired by the speaker, causing
the speaker to fail in gaining a desired goal.

EXAMPLES

3. 雨 の 中 を わざわざ 神田 まで 行ったのに，欲しい 本 は 買え
   Ame no naka o waza-waza *Kanda made   itta   noni,   hoshii hon wa kae-*
   なかった。
   nakatta.

   In the rain I *managed to* make it to Kanda, but was unable to buy the book I wanted.

4. 大切　な 会議 を 欠席 して わざわざ 出掛けた のに，友人 は 留守
   Taisetsu na kaigi o kesseki shite waza-waza *dekaketa noni,   yūjin wa rusu*
   だった。
   datta.

   I *especially* absented myself from the important meeting in order to make a call on my friend, only to find he had gone out.

SECTION C Negative Implication, Indicating Annoyance

In this very common usage, the expression indicates a strong reaction of dislike, and a feeling of annoyance or implied disapproval of the actions of others.

EXAMPLES

5. いやだ と 言う のに，あの人 は わざわざ　私　の 前 でたば
   Iya   da to iu   noni,   ano hito wa waza-waza *watakushi no mae de taba-*
   こ を 吸っている。
   ko o sutte iru.

   Although I said I did not like it, that fellow is *deliberately* smoking in front of me.

6. 最近 は 新しい 服 を わざわざ きたなくして 着ている　若者　が
   Saikin wa atarashii fuku o waza-waza *kitanaku shite   kiteiru wakamono ga*
   いる。
   iru.

   Recently I have seen young people wearing new clothes that they had *purposely* made dirty.

Yahari やはり   too, as well, as expected, still, but then
  Yappari やっぱり

EXPLANATION: Both pronunciations of this expression, **yahari** and
yappari are acceptable, though **yappari** tends to be used in more
informal conversation. The expression indicates a continuity, in the
sense that some prior situation, attitude or condition has not changed
and continues to be true. See Section A. However, the reasons for
this continuity can vary slightly, for example either because of some
basic logic governing the condition or only because of the speaker's
personal prediction.   The slightly differing nuances of this expression are illustrated in Sections B through D.   Its use as a conversational interjection is shown in Section E.

SECTION A   Indicating Continuity
This usage employs the basic meaning of the expression, to indicate
that a prior situation or condition remains the same as before, or
that the prior condition will continue. It indicates that the current
situation is a direct result of the previous situation.

EXAMPLES

1. きのう も 蒸し暑かった が，今日 も やはり 蒸し暑い。
   Kinō   mo mushi-atsukatta ga,   kyō mo yahari *mushi-atsui.*
   It was muggy yesterday, so it is muggy today *too.*

2. 先月　 も 赤字 だったが，今月　 も　やはり 赤字 だ。
   Sengetsu mo akaji datta ga, kongetsu mo yahari *akaji da.*
   They were in the red last month, and they are in the red this
   month *as well.*

SECTION B   Expressing a Logical Outcome
The expression **yahari** can be used to indicate the speaker's prediction that some situation or event will develop in an expected manner
because of some logical chain of reasoning which must apply. It
can be used by itself as a response to someone else, in which case
the speaker is agreeing to the probable outcome of events. For

example, if someone says, "They say that company might go bankrupt this month," an appropriate agreeing answer would be "**yahari**," (They *probably* will).

EXAMPLES

3. 朝 の天気予報で 雨 に なると 言っていたが, やはり 午後 から
    Asa no tenki-yohō de ame ni naru to itte ita ga, yahari *gogo kara*

    雨 が 降り出した。
    ame ga furi-dashita.

    On the morning news they were saying it was likely to rain, and *sure enough* it began to rain in the afternoon.

4. あの 会社 は 大分 前 から景気が よくない よう だったが, やはり
    Ano kaisha wa daibu mae kara keiki ga yoku nai yō datta ga, yahari

    先月　　 倒産 した。
    sengetsu tōsan shita.

    Business has not seemed very good for that company for quite a while, and *as expected* the company went bankrupt last month.

5. A: あの 会社 は 倒産する かも 知れません よ。
    Ano kaisha wa tōsan suru kamo shiremasen yo.

   A: You know, that company may go bankrupt.

   B: やはり。
    Yahari.

   B: *Probably.* (Yes, it *probably* will.)

6. A: 山田さん と 鈴木さん はこの 春　結婚 する そう です よ。
    Yamada-san to Suzuki-san wa kono haru kekkon suru sō desu yo.

   A: I hear Yamada-san and Suzuki-san will get married this spring.

   B: やっぱり。
    Yappari.

   B: *Probably.* (Yes, *I think so.*)

SECTION C Result of Personal Thinking

A common usage of **yahari** is to indicate that the speaker has thought over some issue and, even after thinking it through, continues to have the same opinion as previously. Used in this sense, the expression might be translated as *still*.

EXAMPLES

7. 欠点 も あるが，やはり　　私　　は 彼女 が 好きだ。
   Ketten mo aru ga,　yahari *watakushi wa kanojo ga suki da.*

   In spite of some faults, I *still* like her.

8. 父　　は家業を継げと言うが，やはり　　私　　は 医者 に なろう。
   Chichi wa kagyō o tsuge to iu ga,　yahari *watakushi wa isha ni narō.*

   Father said I should carry on the family business, but I am still *determined* to become a doctor.

SECTION D Development According to Common Sense

Often **yahari** indicates that some situation or condition is developing just as everyone thought it would, based on common sense.

EXAMPLES

9. やはり，日本 の 富士山 は 美しい。
   Yahari, *Nippon no Fujisan wa utsukushii.*

   Japan's Mt. Fuji is, *after all*, beautiful.

10. 日本 の 花 は，やはり　　桜 でしょう。
    Nihon no hana wa,　yahari *sakura deshō.*

    The *typical* Japanese flower is the sakura, isn't it?

SECTION E Conversational *Interjection*

Yahari or **yappari** is used often as a conversational interjection. When used in such a manner its specific meaning is open to many possible translations because it is, strictly speaking, not absolutely necessary to the meaning of the sentence, except to the degree that it helps the flow of conversation. Any one of the possible nuances illustrated above might be implied in the interjection, though not necessarily only those given above.

EXAMPLES

11. 休日　　ですか，やっぱりうちで テレビ なんか みている ことが
    Kyūjitsu desu ka,　yappari *uchi de terebi nanka mite iru koto ga*

多い です。
ōi   desu.

On holidays I *usually* stay home and do things like watch
television.

12. すきな映画は，やはり ミュージカル です ね。
    Suki na eiga wa, yahari *myūjikaru   desu ne.*

    Well, when it comes to films, I like musicals best.

Yatara ni   やたらに   recklessly, rashly, carelessly,
randomly, disorderly

EXPLANATION: The basic meaning of this expression is *carelessly*
and *disorderly,* and by extension it means something done *haphaz-
ardly, randomly* or *rashly.*   It gives a sense of the opposite of anything that is precisely, purposefully or carefully done.

EXAMPLES

1. この 辺 はやたらに 家 が 建って， 緑 がほとんど なくなって しま
   Kono hen wa yatara ni *ie ga tatte, midori ga hotondo   nakunatte shima-*
   った。
   tta.

   Homes were *recklessly* put up in this area, and now there is
   almost no green left.

2. いくら好きでも， そう やたらに 酒を 飲んでは 体 によくあ
   *Ikura suki demo,   sō   *yatara ni *sake o   nonde wa karada ni yoku a-*
   りません よ。
   rimasen   yo.

   Eventhough you like it, it's not good for you to drink *so much*
   sake.

3. 彼 は「やっぱり」と 言う 言葉を 覚えた ばかり で，この 頃 やたら
   Kare wa "yappari" to iu kotoba o oboeta bakari de, kono goro yatara
   に 使っている。
   ni *tsukatte iru.*

   Since he has just learned the word "yappari," he uses it *too*
   often.

Yatto やっと   finally, at last, just, barely, scarcely, only

EXPLANATION: This expression carries with it a slight feeling of
hesitancy, delay, or the presence of a limiting factor. For example,
as shown in Section A, it indicates that after a long period of time
or after a lengthy process, some desired goal has *at last* been reached.
As explained in Sections B and C, it can refer to a goal which was
just *barely* reached, again indicating a feeling of hesitancy. In both
usages there is, behind the surface meaning of the expression, a lack
of certainty that the goal would be reached, and an unenthusiastic
acknowledgement that it has *finally* been reached.

SECTION A   At Last

When used as illustrated below, **yatto** gives the feeling of being set
free from some restrictions or of being set free from anxiety. It
conveys the sense that after a long period of time, or after some
difficulties, a desired goal has *finally* or *at long last* been reached.

EXAMPLES

1. 厳しく　つらい　訓練期間　が やっと 終った。
   Kibishiku tsurai kunren-kikan ga yatto *owatta.*

   The period of strict training was *finally* over.

2. 成人式　を迎えて，子どもっぽかった　娘　がやっとおとならしく
   Seijin-shiki o mukaete,   kodomoppokatta musume ga yatto   *otona rashiku*
   なった。
   natta.

   With the coming-of-age ceremony my daughter, who had been
   so child-like, *at last* began to act like a woman. (Note that the
   use of *yatto* in this sentence implies that the speaker had some
   concern about his daughter and felt perhaps she was late in
   learning to act as an adult. Every year in Japan on 15 January
   coming-of-age ceremonies and parties are held throughout the
   country to honor those who have just reached the age of twenty,
   which is considered to mark their change into the status of an
   adult.)

3. いつも すれ違い だった ふたり が，六年後 に やっと めぐり会えた。
Itsumo sure-chigai datta futari ga, rokunen-go ni yatto *meguri-aeta.*

After six years, those two who had always passed by each other
finally chanced to meet.

SECTION B Just, Barely

Yatto also indicates a condition in which a goal has *just barely* been
reached. Used in this way it refers to the lowest acceptable level
of some condition.

EXAMPLES

4. 彼 の英語は 新聞 が やっと 読める 程度 です。
Kare no Eigo wa shimbun ga yatto *yomeru teido desu.*

His English is *just* good enough to read a newspaper.

5. 少い 収入 で，親子 四人 やっと 生きている。
Sukunai shūnyū de, oya-ko yo-nin yatto *ikite iru.*

The four people, parents and children, *barely* kept alive with a
small income.

6. 希望する 大学 に やっと 補欠 で入れた。
Kibō suru daigaku ni yatto *hoketsu de haireta.*

I just *barely* got into the university I wanted as part of a quota.
《(i.e., the literal meaning is that the person was accepted as an
alternate chosen to fill the quota set by the university.)》

SECTION C Just, Barely (with *desu*)

Yatto can also be used as shown below with the word *desu*, in
which case it carries the same meanings as shown in Section B.

EXAMPLES

7. 私 の 能力 では，予備校 に 入る の が やっと です。
Watakushi no nōryoku de wa, yobikō ni hairu no ga yatto *desu.*

With my abilities I'll *barely* be able to get into a cram school.
(Japan has many preparatory or cram schools which are run as
commercial businesses and are designed to train people to be
able to pass school entrance examinations.) The speaker here
is saying that he probably could not get into a university, and

will only barely be able to get into a preparatory cram school.
A similar nuance is carried by sentence no. 8 below.

8. 私　　　の　能力　では，高校を　卒業　するのがやっとです。
   Watakushi no nōryoku de wa, kōkō o sotsugyō suru no ga yatto *desu.*

   With my low abilities, I'll *barely* be able to graduate from high
   school.

9. この　不況では，従業員　に　給料を払う　のがやっとです。
   Kono fukyō de wa, jūgyōin ni kyūryō o harau no ga yatto *desu.*

   With this business slump I can *scarcely* pay my employees.

10. この　英文　の　　翻訳　は，　一日　　五頁　がやっとです。
    Kono Ei-bun no hon'yaku wa, ichi-nichi go-peiji ga yatto *desu.*

    I can *only* translate five pages a day of this English language
    piece.

Yomoya　よもや　　　surely not,　absolutely not,　impossible,
　　　　　　　　　　　　　not very likely

EXPLANATION:　**Yomoya** is similar in meaning to the Japanese
expression *masaka*. Both have a negative implication and refer to
something or some condition which will not occur, but of the two
yomoya is the stronger and it refers to situations whose occurrence
would be an impossibility. Its negative implication is very definite.

EXAMPLES

1. 将来　日本　が戦争を引き起こすこと　はよもやないだろう。
   Shōrai Nihon ga sensō o hiki-okosu koto wa yomoya *nai darō.*

   Surely Japan will not go to war in the future.

2. よもやあの　人が　　犯人　ではないだろう。
   Yomoya *ano hito ga han'nin de wa nai darō.*

   It is *most unlikely* that he is the criminal.

3. いつも　清潔　な政治を唱えている　彼が，よもや買収されるとは
   Itsumo seiketsu na seiji o tonaete iru kare ga, yomoya *baishū sareru to wa*
   思っても　みなかった。
   omotte mo minakatta.

Since he is always preaching about clean government, I *never suspected* he was a person who could be bought. (I was surprised to hear he was bought.)

Yōyaku　ようやく　　finally, at last

EXPLANATION: **Yōyaku** indicates that some situation is gradually changing after a rather long or slow process has been taking place. It expresses a note of guarded optimism that a future improvement can be hoped for.

EXAMPLES

1. 教えはじめて 三年, 彼 の 発音 は ようやく 日本語 らしく なっ
   Oshie-hajimete san-nen, kare no hatsuon wa yōyaku Nihongo rashiku nat-
   て きた。
   te kita.

   I've been teaching him for three years now, and his pronunciation *finally* sounds like Japanese.

2. ようやく 薬 がきいて きた よう です。 熱 が下って きました。
   Yōyaku kusuri ga kiite kita yō desu. Netsu ga sagatte kimashita.

   At last it seems the medicine has taken effect. The fever has gone down.

3. 発育 が 悪いと 心配 していたけれど, ようやくうちの子も
   Hatsuiku ga warui to shimpai shite ita keredo, yōyaku uchi no ko mo
   歩きはじめた。
   aruki-hajimeta.

   I was worried that our child's development was poor, but *finally* he began to walk.

AFFECTIVE EXPRESSIONS IN JAPANESE
—A Handbook of Value-Laden Words
in Everyday Japanese—
日本語感情表現の手引

1982年9月10日　初版発行　　　1992年7月20日　8刷発行

著　者	Ronald Suleski 政　田　寛　子
発行者	株式 会社 北 星 堂 書 店
	代表者 山 本 雅 三

〒113 東 京 都 文 京 区 本 駒 込 3-32-4
Tel (03) 3827-0511　Fax (03) 3827-0567

検印省略

THE HOKUSEIDO PRESS
32-4, Honkomagome 3-chome, Bunkyo-ku, Tokyo 113 Japan

❖落丁・乱丁本はお取替いたします。